CONCEPTION, CONTRACEPTION:
A New Look

CONCEPTION, CONTRACEPTION:
A New Look

by Suzanne Loebl

McGRAW-HILL BOOK COMPANY
New York   St. Louis   San Francisco
Montreal   Toronto

$6.84
Hunting

Picture appearing on page 8
Courtesy of the Karl-Marx Universität

Pictures appearing on pages 7, 24, 36, 40, 100, 113
Courtesy of the National Library of Medicine, Bethesda, Maryland.

Picture appearing on page 10
Courtesy of the Family Health Foundation, New Orleans, Louisiana.

Pictures appearing on pages 29, 31, 33, 81
Courtesy of Planned Parenthood World Population.

Picture appearing on page 38
Courtesy of Columbia University.

Pictures appearing on pages 43, 45
Courtesy of The New York Academy of Medicine.

Picture appearing on page 63
Courtesy of the Syntex Corporation.

Pictures appearing on pages 66, 70
Courtesy of the Worcester Foundation for Experimental Biology.

Pictures appearing on pages 25, 85, 98
Courtesy of the International Planned Parenthood Association, Western Hemisphere, London.

Picture appearing on page 91
Courtesy of the International Planned Parenthood Association of New York.

Picture appearing on page 121
Courtesy of Ortho Pharmaceuticals.

Designed by Marcy J. Katz

Library of Congress Cataloging in Publicat

Loebl, Suzanne.
    Conception, Contraception: a new look.
    SUMMARY: An introduction for teenager_
control, including information on conception, contraception, and
leaders in the field.
    1. Birth control—Juvenile literature.   [1. Birth
control.   2. Population]   I. Title.   [DNLM:
1. Contraception—Popular works.   2. Family planning
—Popular works.   3. Reproduction—Popular works.
WQ205 L825c 1973]
HQ766.L57   301.32'1   73-8018
ISBN 0-07-038340-5 (lib. bdg.)
ISBN 0-07-038339-1

123456789BPBP7987654

CONTENTS

ACKNOWLEDGMENTS   vii
FOREWORD   ix
1 NO MAN IS AN ISLAND   1
2 CROCODILE DUNG AND BETEL LEAVES   4
3 BIRTH CONTROL BECOMES A
     NATIONAL CAUSE   13
4 "I HAVE PROMISES TO KEEP"   22
5 THE SEARCH FOR THE MAMMALIAN EGG   35
6 PHYSIOLOGY COMES OF AGE   48
7 "I INVENTED THE PILL BECAUSE
     OF A WOMAN"   65
8 A TABOO METHOD COMES INTO ITS OWN   80
9 MALE METHODS   96
10 ABORTION   111
11 NEW DEVELOPMENTS IN CONTRA-
     CEPTION   118
12 THERE WAS AN OLD WOMAN WHO
     LIVED IN A SHOE   126
13 CONCLUSION   139
    BIBLIOGRAPHY   142
    INDEX   143

FOR DAVID WITH
LOVE AND APPRECIATION

Acknowledgments

It may be fitting that a book on conception and contraception had an unusually long pregnancy. The manuscript took shape when the author was an Advanced Science Writing Fellow at the School of Journalism of Columbia University in 1968–69. The University and the Sloan Foundation that supported a large share of the program deserve my thanks, as does program director Kenneth K. Goldstein and my fellow students.

I want to express my gratitude to the many busy scientists whom I interviewed in the course of my research and who often were able to provide firsthand accounts concerning important developments described here: J. Michael Bedford, Samuel Bunker, M. C. Chang, R. J. Ericsson, Alan F. Guttmacher, Hans Lehfeldt, Miriam Menkin, Gerald Oster, John Rock, Sheldon Segal, Victor Sidel, and Christopher Tietze.

One of the great pleasures in writing *Conception, Contraception: A New Look*, was to delve freely into the riches of the past. To list all the books and articles used as background material and for inspiration would be an almost impossible task. Sources used include both primary ones, like the original scientific writings as well as public lectures of those whose story is told here, and secondary ones, like historical accounts, textbooks, review and magazine articles. A selection of the nontechnical material used is presented in the bibliography. My thanks and admiration go to all those on whose work mine is based.

The large excerpts of the autobiography of Margaret Sanger that appear in Chapters 3 and 4 are used by permission of her estate.

I owe a debt of gratitude to Dr. S. Bruce Schearer, staff scientist of the Population Council, who carefully read the entire manuscript and made many helpful suggestions. Though his help cannot be overestimated, I alone am responsible for any possible errors or misinterpretations.

I would like to thank Mrs. Esta Hare for typing the manuscript.

Finally, I would like to thank my family and friends for their support. My children, Judy and David, as usual were valuable junior editors, and my husband, Ernest, provided criticism and encouragement when the going became rough.

Foreword

Conception, Contraception: A New Look by Suzanne Loebl will be of interest not only to mature junior readers, but to social and medical scientists, physicians, administrators, and to anyone interested in population and fertility control. Although it concerns science, the text is so clearly explained that all readers can understand the material.

The history of the population problem and attempts to manage it are clearly stated. A biography of Margaret Sanger includes a vivid description of her struggle to reach her goals and provides Sanger admirers with little-known facts. The development of knowledge concerning the reproductive tracts and their function is carefully traced from the days of speculation to those of scientific fact.

The long and complex events that led to the development of oral hormonal contraception are described with accuracy and in a fascinating manner. The rebirth of the intrauterine devices for contraception is a well-told story, and the advantages as well as the disadvantages of the method are discussed. The need for new methods that men can use is stressed in association with a review of research in progress at several centers.

The United States Supreme Court ruling on abortions is discussed and methods of producing abortion are described. The author notes that most abortions are needed because women do not use contraceptives. An excellent chapter on new developments in contraception provides the reader with information that is not widely available and provides hope for better methods in the near future. Use of any such methods should be with the advice of the reader's physician.

Mrs. Loebl concludes her most interesting book with a chapter relating the concerns of governments with the population problem and notable examples of attempts to decrease growth rates.

Anna L. Southam, M.D.
Program Officer
International Division, Population
The Ford Foundation

CONCEPTION, CONTRACEPTION:
A New Look

1
No Man Is an Island

Can you visualize New York City, or Rio de Janeiro, or Calcutta, or Tokyo with twice today's population?

Can you imagine many more people going to the beach in summer, driving back from vacation, or simply sitting on the grass in front of their houses to catch a breath of fresh air?

Can you imagine twice as many people needing work, wanting to build homes, and using hospitals, schools, buses, incinerator plants? Twice as many people strewing newspapers and soda cans all over?

It seems like a nightmare, but population figures indicate that, even under the best of circumstances, the population of the world will have doubled in thirty-five years.

There will be mass hunger. Half of the people on earth do not get enough to eat already. Even the new wheat and high-protein corn cannot keep up with population growth. Efforts at increasing food production with pesticides and artificial fertilizers are backfiring, and we are beginning to lose some of the birds, fish, and other creatures that share this planet with us.

And then there is energy. Until about a hundred years ago, man contented himself with cutting trees and digging coal from near the surface of the earth. Then came oil and electricity, cars and other machines that devour energy at a rapid rate. Today civilization is threatened simultaneously by an acute fuel shortage and by pollution, both consequences of "high living."

Concrete problems of food, energy, and pollution are only part of the picture. We once thought that man and other animals needed only food and shelter to survive. But laboratory experiments have shown that even rats need a certain amount of space in order to behave according to their customary pattern. In spite of all possible creature comforts, a rat society breaks down completely when the population exceeds a certain density. Animals attack one another, the females give birth prematurely and neglect or devour their young, the males band together in small roving groups, dominated by a strong leader, and engage in homosexuality.

Sometimes, when I am afraid to venture onto the city streets at night, or when I read of the senseless crimes committed by my fellow creatures, I wonder whether we already have reached the human equivalent of overcrowded rats.

Of course, I am not always unhappy or worried. I do escape the city once in a while, to walk in the woods with the trees as my only companions, to sun on an uncrowded beach, or to look at the star-studded sky through a still clear atmosphere.

I even love the city, with its museums, its theaters, and the mixture of humanity that mingles on its streets.

And I love the two healthy children I am fortunate to have. Often, I wish I had more than two, for they are my only claim to immortality, and wouldn't my claim be more secure if I had ten instead of two?

But the time of humanity's unlimited growth is long past. Figures about the population explosion have become so commonplace that they have ceased to be impressive. There were less than one billion human beings on the earth in 1830. One hundred years later there were two billion. Now there are three and a half billion. By the year 2000 there will be seven billion, and the addition of the next billion will take five years or less. *If* population growth at the present rate continues, we will be packed like sardines in six hundred years (there will then be one person per square foot of dry land), and in seventeen hundred years (less time than the Christian

2

Era) the weight of the people will exceed the total weight of the earth. Obviously such a growth rate cannot continue indefinitely; the only question is how and when it will be halted—voluntarily and *now,* before it is too late; or involuntarily through famines, disease, or other catastrophes.

Gloomy predictions about overpopulation have existed since Thomas Malthus' days, 175 years ago, but were almost entirely ignored. Fortunately, those in power have at last awakened. Twelve years after President Eisenhower declared that family planning was entirely a private matter, another Republican President appointed a commission that studied the impact of population growth on the American future.

The question of population growth is complex. It used to be believed that when people were provided with one or several simple and inexpensive methods of contraception, the birth rate would automatically drop to a safe level.

This has proved false. Until very recently, the affluent have used birth control to space their children, but have still chosen a reproductive rate that is too high. The deprived, by choice or by necessity, have continued to act as if "children were the riches of the poor."

Even though adequate methods of birth control are only part of the answer to overpopulation, mankind's long search for such techniques is the subject of this book. Contraceptive research suddenly has become fashionable; contraception, however, is an old concern. At this point in history it is interesting and instructive to look at what is known already, to find out how that knowledge was acquired, and to learn why modern contraceptive methods work, and more important still, why it is so difficult to find "the perfect contraceptive."

In most parts of the world overpopulation is the number one health problem. In the past, population was kept in check by disease, famine, and other outside factors. Today every one of us bears personal responsibility for the fate of generations to come.

2
Crocodile Dung and Betel Leaves

Boccaccio, in his *Decameron,* tells how the hermit Rustico could have his way with a devout but simple-minded maiden by showing her how to perform the pious act of putting his "devil" into her "hell."

The *Decameron* was written six hundred years ago, but even today there are women who, if they are not actually ignorant of how babies are made, are unable to avoid unplanned pregnancies. When Dr. Joseph Diehl Beasley surveyed the beliefs and practices of a cross section of Louisiana citizens in 1964, he found that many women were unaware of the most elementary facts of human reproduction. About one-third of those interviewed did not know that pregnancy resulted from the union of sperm and egg. Among the poor, less than 20 percent of the women knew that the chance of becoming pregnant follows a rhythmical pattern, or at what time of the month they were most likely to conceive. The contraceptive practices used included douches made of cola and aspirin or diluted potash. These methods are not far removed from the fourteen live tadpoles Chinese women were advised to swallow three days after menstruation, or the tube filled with cat liver that

4

Byzantine brides attached to their left foot so as to avoid conception.

A quick glance at the population figures of the United States and the rest of the world indicates that the poor have more children than the rich, nonwhites more than whites, the unskilled more than the skilled.

Contrary to popular belief, these differences are not a matter of choice, biology, or attitude. Time and again it has been shown that practically all women want to have control over the when and how of motherhood, and when Beasley opened his first birth-control clinic in rural Lincoln Parish, Louisiana, patients came on opening night even though hurricane-force winds were rattling the windowpanes and the town had been blacked out by a power failure.

Not surprisingly perhaps, Dr. Beasley is a pediatrician, and it was his concern with the hopeless state of his young charges that turned him into a crusader for contraception. As he said recently: "In all our efforts to rescue ghetto dwellers, the school dropouts, the functional illiterates, it seemed to me that we have been applying technology to space and commercial problems while failing dismally to apply it to human problems."

To the best of his ability, the young doctor—he was thirty-five at the time—was to remedy this omission in Louisiana. Since the state had never before allowed birth-control information to be freely available, Joe Beasley could start from scratch. His clinics now rely on computers, flow charts, cost accounting, and all the other managerial techniques so successfully used by big business, but these impersonal aids are hidden behind the scenes. At the clinic each patient is treated like a welcome guest. The staff is courteous and attentive, and has ample time to listen to individual problems. Reception rooms are clean and cheerful, dressing rooms are private, and waiting time is reduced to a minimum.

But the clinic does more than counsel those who show up on their own. It provides baby-sitting and transportation and actively seeks out potential patients in the community. New mothers are contacted in the hospital, and "high risk" women, identified from health records, are visited at home. The why and how of missed appointments are investigated within a day or two, for it has been proved that such speedy action motivates 68 percent of the women to keep subsequent ones, instead of the 28 percent who would show when the follow-up was delayed by two weeks.

5

Such attention to detail has already paid off. Ninety-two percent of all patients returned for their next scheduled appointment, for as one woman said, "Everybody's so nice that you just feel like coming back."

The positive attitude on the part of the staff is unusual, for contraception, traditionally, has been the most neglected aspect of medicine, more so even than childbirth itself.

The spacing of children has long been considered desirable. Yet, even today, more than 50 percent of all physicians fail to discuss contraception with new mothers during the customary post partum (after childbirth) examination, a time at which a woman is most receptive to such advice.

This indifference on the part of health personnel has never kept people from trying to limit the number of their offspring, though these attempts were not always successful. Some form of contraception has been practiced by all known societies, and records thereof have come down to us in the Bible, medical papyruses, and other documents.

Contraceptive measures fall into three categories. The first uses medicines that, when taken orally, are supposed to make the woman infertile; the second relies on mechanical barriers or techniques designed to prevent the union of sperm and egg; and the third aims at scheduling intercourse during naturally occurring infertile periods of the female.

Though oral contraceptives were completely ineffectual until recently, the variety of concoctions that have been swallowed by women to this end are almost legion.

The Chinese, in A.D. 695, recommended "quicksilver [mercury], fried for a whole day in oil." A piece of this, the size of a small lozenge and swallowed on an empty stomach, would prevent the taker from ever becoming pregnant. Other poisons, like strychnine, lead, and arsenic, were recommended at other times in history. The Greeks believed in eating the uterus of a she-goat, whereas Moroccan women preferred mule flesh—for is not the mule a sterile animal? The Hindus, as always, were partial to plants, and the Eddystone Islanders wrapped a mixture of nuttree bark and a certain kind of reddish stone into a betel leaf. Since they must have had some doubts about the effectiveness of the formulation, they enhanced its power by chanting: "I make this woman here eat betel; let her be as the stone of the mountain; let her not make a child; let her be barren."

6

AD 1550

• JUGOSLAVIJA — POLENŠAK

BEFORE GOING TO THE MARRIAGE CEREMONY THE BRIDE PUT AN UNLOCKED PADLOCK INTO THE BODICE OF HER DRESS. SHE DECIDED UPON THE NUMBER OF HER CHILDLESS YEARS BY MAKING THE SAME NUMBER OF STEPS OUTSIDE HER HOUSE WITH THE PADLOCK UNLOCKED, THEN SHE LOCKED IT.

AD 1600

• JUGOSLAVIJA — PAVLOVCI AT ORMOŽ

WHEN THE BRIDE—GROOM CAME TO TAKE THE BRIDE TO THE MARRIAGE CEREMONY, SHE CLIMBED UP A LADDER AS MANY RUNGS AS SHE WANTED TO HAVE CHILDREN IN HER WEDLOCK.

AD 1650

• JUGOSLAVIJA — ČRNI VRH ABOVE IDRIJA

WOMEN REMAINED CHILDLESS THE SAME NUMBER OF YEARS AS WAS THAT OF THE BARLEY GRAINS THROWN INTO THEIR WEDDING SHOES.

Birth control advice for a Medieval bride.

Ancient Egyptian medical papyruses list contraceptive prescriptions.
The "Ebers" papyrus describes a medicated tampon for insertion into the vagina.

Oral contraceptives and magic incantations never worked, at least not for their intended purpose. Mechanical barriers, introduced into the vagina and designed to block the entrance to the womb, were more effective. To this end the Egyptians, in 1850 B.C., recommended fashioning a paste of crocodile dung, the Jews advocated a sponge, and the Greeks a piece of soft wool or a mixture made of sour oil, honey, and cedar gum.

Methods based on the temporal variations in fertility of the woman were more successful than the old antifertility compounds and less so than mechanical means.

It has always been known that women are less likely to conceive while breast-feeding, a function that often delays the resumption of ovulation. Even though prolonged lactation is unreliable as a means of birth control, it is still widely practiced throughout the world. It can, however, be used only after a woman has given birth. Long before anyone even started to search for the mammalian egg, it was also known that women are more likely to conceive during some parts of the month than during others. The fertility pattern of the menstrual cycle has consequently been utilized to regulate birth, and even today the rhythm method is the only contraceptive practice officially sanctioned by the Roman Catholic Church.

Cultures that set great stock by high birth rates, on the other hand, instituted measures that were designed to maximize conception. The Talmud, for example, insisted on abstention until a woman had gone to the *mikvah*, the purifying bath, one week after her period. In this way intercourse was likely to take place when the woman was most fertile and the man had a large reserve of sperm.

The rhythm method never worked very well for birth-control purposes. Prior to the nineteenth century the timing of the safe period was a matter of trial and error, and even after the ovulation cycle was discovered, scientists believed the time of ovulation coincided with menstruation. The "safe period" was thus scheduled in the middle of the month. Actually, menstruation and ovulation are the two poles of the menstrual cycle. The ovum is released from the ovary twelve to sixteen days before menstruation, and the "period" itself is proof of the fact that the soft lining the uterus had prepared for "nidation," or nesting of the fertilized egg, is now superfluous and must be sloughed off.

Dr. Joseph D. Beasley counseling a patient at the Family Health Foundation in Louisiana.

10

The understanding of the menstrual cycle led to a somewhat more reliable rhythm method based on the reading of the calendar, or more recently on a careful daily record of the body temperature, which changes with ovulation. The safe period is now considered to extend to within three to four days on either side of ovulation. Even with this more exact knowledge, however, the method only works for women who are very careful and regular.

When Dr. Beasley opened the doors of his clinic in Louisiana, he was fortunate in that he could offer his patients a choice of contraceptive measures. These included the traditional ones, such as the diaphragm and rhythm, and modern ones, such as IUD's and oral contraceptives. Soon, these may be outdated and replaced by even better or safer ones.

To be effective, contraceptive measures must act on the key points of the reproductive process. Some of these are obvious, like the union of sperm and ovum. Others, like those governed by hormones, were discovered comparatively recently. Others are still only possibilities on the scientific drawing board. These include prevention of the rupture of the follicle, changes in the uterine lining, action on the transport system of the sperm cells or of the egg, a better way to pinpoint ovulation, or any other method that alters one of the numerous steps necessary to create one new creature from the fusion of two individual cells.

Contraceptive practice is very old, but a concentrated effort at developing scientific methods is very new. It has already paid off. The Pill, whose safe use for long periods of time is questioned today, is about fifteen years old, and a widespread search for more effective IUD is even more recent. At this rate of development, we can look forward to a rapid increase in the available methods of birth control.

Any method that is discovered will probably serve double duty. It will help the fertile to limit their progeny and the infertile to become parents, for as John Rock, one of the three fathers of the Pill, has said, "With the discovery of how to establish conception when conception is desired, we shall unavoidably learn how to prevent it when that is desirable. The physiology involved in both problems is the same."

Contraception, however, is much more than a strictly scientific, medical, or even educational problem. The government and the church have long felt that they had the right to regulate the outcome of the sex life of their citizens and flock. Before birth-control information could become freely available, the laws of the land and the attitude of those in power had to be changed.

In the United States this task was accomplished almost single-handedly by Margaret Sanger, a resolute young nurse who, like Dr. Beasley exactly fifty years later, felt that "she was through with half-way, clandestine measures" and was determined to get at the root of the problem.

3
Birth Control Becomes a National Cause

It is fitting that the birth-control movement in America was created by a woman. Since the name of Margaret Sanger was synonymous with contraception for more than a quarter of a century, she must be part of any book on the subject.

Fortunately for those whose cause she was to espouse, Margaret Sanger was endowed with the gift of the pen. It was through her medical column in The *Call,* a Socialist newspaper of the day, that she first attracted attention, and the various books, journals, and pamphlets she wrote during her long life were often her only steady source of income. Since she told her own story better than anyone else, I too shall use her words wherever possible.

Margaret Sanger was a born crusader and revolutionary. She probably inherited her indignation from her father, Michael Hennessey Higgins, who at thirteen ran away from his home in Canada to join Lincoln's army. Young Higgins had to wait a year and a half before he was old enough to enlist, and when he did he fought valiantly, being one of the three men of his regiment to be commended by General Sherman for bravery. In spite of this honor, he was appalled by the horror of war, and for the rest of his life he was content to fight with words. Michael Higgins was a sculptor, making a meager living carving angels out of marble. These were used to decorate the cemeteries in and around Corning, New York. His radical ideas angered the local priest and without his patronage the family income, which had never been plentiful, dwindled. As Margaret recalled later:

Christmases were on the poverty line. If any of us needed a new winter overcoat or pair of overshoes, these constituted our presents. I was the youngest of six, but after me others kept coming until we were eleven. Our dolls were babies—living, wriggling bodies to bathe and dress instead of lifeless faces that never cried or slept. A pine beside the door was our Christmas tree. Father liked us to use natural things and we had to rely upon ingenuity rather than village stores, so we decorated it with white popcorn and red cranberries which we strung ourselves. Our most valuable gift was that of imagination.

Even as an adult Margaret Sanger could not forget the poverty of her childhood and the urge to take that which one does not have. When she was eight *Uncle Tom's Cabin* was performed at the Corning Opera House—admission was ten cents. Margaret had come without the required dime, hoping that a miracle would see her inside the theater.

The throng at the entrance grew thicker and thicker. Curtain time had almost come, and still no miracle. Nevertheless, I simply had to get into that theater. All about me had tickets or money or both. Suddenly I felt something touch my arm—the purse of a woman who was pressed close beside me. It was open, and I could see the coveted coins within. One quick move and I could have my heart's desire. The longing was so deep and hard that it blotted out everything except my imperative need. I *had* to get into that theater.

Margaret was saved from stealing by a sudden movement of the crowd that bore her past the ticket taker. But she could not forget how close she had come to faltering and she did not enjoy the play. She later resolved to start on a regimen of self-fortification so as to withstand temptation in the future. Her program included going to bed upstairs without a light, to the cellar without singing, or jumping off the rafters of the barn onto a haystack thirty feet below.

Early in life she also became convinced that wealth and small families went hand in hand:

Corning was not on the whole a pleasant town. Along the river flats lived the factory workers, chiefly Irish; on the heights above the rolling clouds of smoke that belched from the chimneys lived the owners and executives. The tiny yards of the former were a-sprawl with children; in the gardens on the hills only two or three played. This contrast made a track in my mind. Large families were associated with poverty, toil, unemployment, drunkenness, cruelty, fighting, jails; the small ones with cleanliness, leisure, freedom, light, space, sunshine.

In spite of the strained finances of the Higgins family, Margaret went to Claverack College, a boarding school near Hudson, New York. Here she first demonstrated her ability for leadership. Annoyed at the strict rules of the campus she persuaded six of her fellow students to climb out of a window and spend an evening on the town. The next morning she was called in by Mr. Flack, the director of the school.

Miss Higgins, don't you feel rather ashamed of yourself for getting these girls into trouble last night, by taking them out and making them break the rules? They may even have to be sent home.

Margaret was surprised that the director had singled her out for punishment. Someone, no doubt, must have told on her. Her suspicion was dispelled, however, when Mr. Flack continued:

I don't need to be told that you must have been the ringleader. Again and again I've noticed your influence over others. I want to call your attention to this, because I know you're going to use it in the future. You must make your choice—whether to get yourself and others into difficulty, or else guide yourself and others into constructive activities which will do you and them credit.

Margaret had the rare wisdom of listening to Mr. Flack, and years later she thanked him for having offered guidance instead of discipline.

After three happy years at Claverack, Margaret Higgins took up teaching. This career was short-lived. After a few months her father summoned her home to nurse her mother, who was dying of TB. At her bedside Margaret became engrossed in medical books and resolved to become a doctor. But the enormous gap that separated Claverack College and medical school had to be bridged. As a start she enrolled as a student nurse at White Plains Hospital in White

Plains, New York. She was trained in all branches of nursing, but soon realized that for her the birth of a child held the greatest meaning:

To see a baby born is one of the greatest experiences that a human being can have. Birth to me has always been more awe-inspiring than death. As often as I have witnessed the miracle, held the perfect creature with its tiny hands and tiny feet, each time I have felt as though I were entering a cathedral with prayer in my heart.

It was during this period of her life that she met Bill Sanger, an architect. After a short courtship they were married and moved to St. Nicholas Avenue and 149th Street in New York City. The neighborhood, which today is part of Harlem, was then on the outskirts of town. The Sangers' happiness was soon clouded. While nursing her mother Margaret had contracted TB, and now there was serious concern for her own life. Her first child, Stuart, was born "at home" in New York City, but within weeks Margaret Sanger returned to a sanatorium in Saranac, New York. Hopelessness engulfed her. She did not care what happened to Bill or Stuart, whether she ate, or where she was going to spend the remaining few months of her life. Before she was sent to another sanatorium one of the two doctors who had taken care of her came to see her. "Don't be like this!" he said, "Don't let yourself get into such a mental condition. Do something! Want something! You'll never get well if you keep on this way."

These words electrified Margaret Sanger. Instead of moving to the new sanatorium, she returned to St. Nicholas Avenue. Bill, who had received two contradictory telegrams in one day—one saying that his wife was going to Saranac, the other asking him to meet her train at Grand Central Station—was puzzled, but said as he greeted her at the station, "You did just the right thing. I won't let you die."

Within months the Sangers moved to Hastings-on-Hudson. They had two more children and spent a few happy years in that New York suburb. But they felt drawn to the life of the nearby sprawling city and in 1910 they returned to Manhattan.

The demand for reform swept America, and the Sangers became involved in the Socialist movement—attending discussion meetings several evenings a week. At these, the woman who later was to speak to and for thousands, would murmur her questions and comments to Bill, who announced, "Margaret has something to say on that. Have you heard Margaret?" Then Margaret would put her ideas forth.

Once during these early years, her friend Anita Bloch, editor of the women's page of *The Call*, prevailed on Margaret to take over a women's meeting for which at the last minute she could not find a speaker. Margaret complied, but with fear:

Shaking and quaking I faced my little handful of women who had come after their long working hours for enlightenment. Since I did not consider myself qualified to speak on labor, I switched the subject to health, with which I was more familiar. This, it appeared, was something new.

Margaret spoke about contraception, venereal disease, and other sex-related health problems. The audience was pleased and demanded more such talks, and at the next meeting her audience had swelled to seventy-five. The questions on health and on "intimate family life" were so numerous that it was decided that Margaret Sanger should write a series of articles for *The Call*. Thus it was that she embarked on her mission.

A few weeks after she started writing for *The Call* she saw that one column, which dealt with gonorrhea and syphilis, had been obliterated with black letters:

WHAT EVERY GIRL SHOULD KNOW

N
O
T
H
I
N
G
!

BY ORDER OF
THE POST-OFFICE DEPARTMENT

Margaret Sanger had had her first run-in with the Comstock Law, which had protected the "morals" of the United States for several decades.

Anthony Comstock, head of the Society for the Suppression of Vice, had pushed this law through a busy Congress on the eve of its adjournment in 1873. The Comstock Law made the importing, mailing, or transport in interstate commerce of "obscene literature" and of any article of medicine for the prevention of conception, or for causing abortion, a criminal offense.

It had been left to the Post Office to decide what literature would be considered lewd, lascivious, indecent, or obscene, and for forty years Anthony Comstock and his society were powerful enough to exercise complete control of the Post Office and thus of the mail of ninety million Americans.

Margaret Sanger's family and her political activities did not keep her from practicing her craft. During the early part of this century women usually gave birth at home, assisted by a doctor, midwife, or nurse. Since this type of work fitted in with her busy schedule, Margaret Sanger often accepted maternity cases. Soon most of her calls came from the Lower East Side in Manhattan.

Once the site of an Indian village outside the walls of New Amsterdam, the Lower East Side had become the gateway of successive waves of new Americans arriving from the ghettos and slums of Europe or Latin America. Life on the Lower East Side was hard and dreary. Margaret Sanger recalled it thirty years later in her autobiography:

The utmost depression came over me as I approached this surreptitious region. Below Fourteenth Street I seemed to be breathing a different air, to be in another world and country where the people had habits and customs alien to anything I had ever heard about.

There were then approximately ten thousand apartments in New York into which no sun ray penetrated directly; such windows as they had opened only on a narrow court from which rose fetid odors. It was seldom cleaned, though garbage and refuse often went down into it. All these dwellings were pervaded by the foul breath of poverty, that moldy, indefinable, indescribable smell which cannot be fumigated out, sickening to me but apparently unnoticed by those who lived there. When I set to work with antiseptics, their pungent sting, at least temporarily, obscured the stench. . . .

Pregnancy was a chronic condition among the women. . . . Suggestions as to what to do for a girl who was "in trouble" or a married woman who was "caught" passed from mouth to mouth—herb teas, turpentine, steaming, rolling downstairs, inserting slippery elm, knitting needles, shoehooks. . . . The doomed women implored me to reveal the "secret" rich people had, offering to pay me extra to tell them; many really believed I was holding information back for money. They asked everybody and tried anything, but nothing did them any good. On Saturday nights I have seen groups of from fifty to one hundred with their shawls over their heads waiting outside the office of a five-dollar abortionist. . . .

[The better-educated segments of the population had access to safer abortions. Many practiced withdrawal. The use of condoms was also widespread. Dr. Alan Guttmacher, president of Planned Parenthood-World Population, remembers coming upon condoms in his home soon after the turn of the century, when he was six years old. He was told at the time that they were finger cots.]

Then one stifling mid-July day of 1912 I was summoned to a Grand Street tenement. My patient was a small, slight Russian Jewess, about twenty-eight years old, of the special cast of feature to which suffering lends a madonna-like expression. The cramped three-room apartment was in a sorry state of turmoil. Jake Sachs, a truck driver scarcely older than his wife, had come home to find the three children crying and her unconscious from the effects of a self-induced abortion. He had called the nearest doctor, who in turn had sent for me. . . .

The doctor and I settled ourselves to the task of fighting the septicemia [blood poisoning resulting from an infection]. Never had I worked so fast, never so concentratedly. The sultry days and nights were melted into a torpid inferno. It did not seem possible there could be such heat, and every bit of food, ice, and drugs had to be carried up three flights of stairs. . . .

After a fortnight Mrs. Sachs' recovery was in sight. Neighbors, ordinarily fatalistic as to the results of abortion, were genuinely pleased that she had survived. . . .

At the end of three weeks, as I was preparing to leave the fragile patient to take up her difficult life once more, she finally voiced her fears, "Another baby will finish me, I suppose?"

"It's too early to talk about that," I temporized.

But when the doctor came to make his last call, I drew him aside. "Mrs. Sachs is terribly worried about having another baby."

"She well may be," replied the doctor, and then he stood before her and said, "Any more such capers, young woman, and there'll be no need to send for me."

"I know, doctor," she replied timidly, "but," and she hesitated as though it took all her courage to say it, "what can I do to prevent it?"

The doctor was a kindly man, and he had worked hard to save her, but such incidents had become so familiar to him that he had long since lost whatever delicacy he might once have had. He laughed good-naturedly.

"You want to have your cake and eat it too, do you? Well, it can't be done."

Then picking up his hat and bag to depart he said, "Tell Jake to sleep on the roof."

I glanced quickly at Mrs. Sachs. Even through my sudden tears I could see stamped on her face an expression of absolute despair. We simply looked at each other, saying no word until the door had closed behind the doctor. Then she lifted her thin, blue-veined hands and clasped them beseechingly. "He can't understand. He's only a man. But you do, don't you? Please tell me the secret, and I'll never breathe it to a soul. *Please!*"

What was I to do? I could not speak the conventionally comforting phrases which would be of no comfort. Instead, I made her as physically easy as I could and promised to come back in a few days to talk with her again. A little later, when she slept, I tiptoed away.

Night after night the wistful image of Mrs. Sachs appeared before me. I made all sorts of excuses to myself for not going back. I was busy on other cases; I really did not know what to say to her or how to convince her of my own ignorance; I was helpless to avert such monstrous atrocities. Time rolled by and I did nothing.

The telephone rang one evening three months later, and Jake Sachs' agitated voice begged me to come at once; his wife was sick again and from the same cause. For a wild moment I thought of sending someone else, but actually, of course, I hurried into my uniform, caught up my bag, and started out. All the way I longed for a subway wreck, an explosion, anything to keep me from having to enter that home again. But nothing happened, even to delay me. I turned into the dingy doorway and climbed the familiar stairs once more. The children were there, young little things.

Mrs. Sachs was in a coma and died within ten minutes. I folded her still hands across her breast, remembering how they had pleaded with me, begging so humbly for the knowledge which was her right. I drew a sheet over her pallid face. Jake was sobbing, running his hands through his hair and pulling it out like an insane person. Over and over again he wailed, "My God! My God! My God!"

I left him pacing desperately back and forth, and for hours I myself walked and walked through the hushed streets. When I finally arrived home and let myself quietly in, all the household was sleeping. I looked out my window and down upon the dimly lighted city. Its pains and griefs crowded in upon me, a moving picture rolled before my eyes with photographic clearness: women writhing in travail to bring forth little babies; the babies themselves naked and hungry, wrapped in newspapers to keep them from the cold; six-year-old children with pinched, pale, wrinkled faces, old in concentrated wretchedness, pushed into gray and fetid cellars, crouching on stone floors, their small scrawny hands scuttling through rags, making lamp shades, artificial flowers; white coffins, black coffins, coffins, coffins interminably passing in never-ending succession. The scenes piled one upon another on another. I could bear it no longer.

As I stood there the darkness faded. The sun came up and threw its reflection over the house tops. It was the dawn of a new day in my life also. The doubt and questioning, the experimenting and trying, were now to be put behind me. I knew I could not go back merely to keeping people alive.

I went to bed, knowing that no matter what it might cost, I was finished with palliatives and superficial cures; I was resolved to seek out the root of evil, to do something to change the destiny of mothers whose miseries were vast as the sky.

4

"I Have Promises to Keep"

—Margaret Sanger

Mrs. Sachs was Margaret Sanger's last professional case. From now on she would search for ways of avoiding such senseless death. As a first step the Sanger family sailed for Europe. Bill longed to devote himself fulltime to painting, Margaret wanted to study birth-control methods in France, a country whose population figures indicated that its women obviously knew how to limit their families. The means to accomplish this, Mrs. Sanger discovered, was handed down from mother to daughter as if it were a precious recipe. The women, however, gladly shared their secret with her. After a three-month stay Margaret gathered her three children, and the little formulas culled from French peasant women, and returned home without her husband, unaware that her parting from him would eventually be permanent.

Back home in New York City she decided to challenge Comstock and his law with two publications. The first, a monthly called *The*

Woman Rebel, with the slogan "No Gods, No Masters," was a call to arms to oppressed womanhood. The second, *Family Limitation,* contained all the information on pessaries, douches, suppositories, and sponges that she had collected in France. For contraceptive purposes a pessary is usually a cap or diaphragm that fits over the cervix. Some of the earlier models had a stem that fitted into the cervical canal and anchored the device more firmly. Douches are meant to flush out sperm after intercourse. Suppositories contain spermicidal, or sperm-killing, agents, and sponges—one of the oldest methods of birth control—absorb sperm and keep them from traveling farther.

Distribution of the publication would mean a jail sentence, but before it could be distributed it had to be printed, and even for the printer it was a "Sing-Sing job." Many refused, but finally she found a man willing to do it—at night, when his shop was supposedly closed. One hundred thousand copies of *Family Limitation,* which was to become the Bible of the birth-control movement were printed, and then hidden to await distribution.

Long before they were in the hands of potential users, their author had been booked on charges of violating the Comstock Law with *The Woman Rebel.* Margaret Sanger knew that she would receive a stiff jail sentence. Since she had not been granted enough time to prepare an adequate defense, she decided on the eve of her arraignment to flee to England, which had just been plunged into World War I. Margaret Sanger was extremely homesick and lonely during her self-imposed exile, but misery did not keep her from spending days, weeks, and months in the library of the British Museum. She also formed lifelong friendships with the philosopher Havelock Ellis and the leaders of the Neo-Malthusian League, the British birth-control movement.

The organization took its name from Thomas Robert Malthus, "the gloomy parson," who as long ago as 1798 had predicted that the world would outgrow its food supply. Malthus argued:

The power of population is indefinitely greater than the power in the earth to produce subsistence for Man. Population, when unchecked, increases in a geometric ratio (1, 2, 4, 8, 16, 32, 64, 128, 256, 512 . . .), while food increases only in an arithmetic progression (1, 2, 3 . . .).

No limits whatever are placed to the productions of the earth; they may increase forever and be greater than any assignable quantity; yet still the

Thomas Malthus

power of population being a power of superior order, the increase of the human species can only be kept commensurate to the increase of the means of subsistence, by the constant operation of the strong law of necessity acting as a check upon the greater power."

Though Margaret Sanger studied Malthus' writings at the British Museum, it was the population figures of Holland that captured her imagination. In this tiny kingdom the maternal death rate and infant mortality were lower than anywhere else in Europe or in the United States. Birth and death rates had declined by a third over the past twenty-five years.

Turn-of-the-century birth-control devices.

Margaret Sanger realized that "the Dutch had long since adopted a common-sense attitude on the subject, looking upon having a baby as an economic luxury—something like a piano or an automobile that had to be taken care of afterwards."

In spite of the mines that infested the North Sea, Margaret Sanger went to Holland to see for herself how this change had been brought about. The spectacular results were due largely to the efforts of Drs. Aletta Jacobs and Johannes Rutgers. Dr. Jacobs, herself the eighth child of a poor physician, was Holland's first woman doctor and, in 1878, the founder of her country's first free clinic for poor women and children. Stillbirths and abortions dropped so dramatically in the vicinity of the clinic that thirty-four of Dr. Jacobs' colleagues founded the Dutch Neo-Malthusian League a few years later. By 1914 the country had fifty such free maternal health clinics.

Dissatisfied with existing methods of birth control, Dr. Jacobs, together with a German gynecologist, Wilhelm Mensinga, developed a diaphragm in 1885 that was eventually adopted throughout the world. Margaret Sanger did not meet personally with Dr. Jacobs, but she was received with open arms by Dr. Rutgers, a smiling, kindly man who had found that proper spacing of children was the secret of healthier mothers and healthier babies: "The numbers in a family or the numbers in a nation might be increased just as long as the arrival of children was not too rapid to permit those already born to be assured of a livelihood and to become assimilated in the community."

Dr. Rutgers invited his guest to the clinic where he fitted women with diaphragms. To her great surprise she learned that he relied on fifteen different types of contraceptives and that the Mensinga diaphragm alone came in fourteen sizes.

Her suitcase crammed with contraceptive material, Margaret returned to the United States in the autumn of 1915. She immediately informed her prosecutor that she was back and ready to stand trial. The mood of the land had changed somewhat in her absence. Feminist groups came to her support, and Clarence Darrow offered to travel to New York and defend her case free of charge.

Margaret Sanger, however, insisted on pleading her case and her cause unaided. The government decided otherwise. After several postponements the case was dismissed for lack of prosecution. Her friends rejoiced, but Margaret Sanger knew that the battle was far from over.

To win others to her cause, she embarked on a cross-country lecture tour. Shy by nature, she was terrified of speaking in public. For weeks she practiced her lecture among the chimney pots on the roof of her Lexington Avenue hotel. When she finally appeared before her first audience, her listeners, who had been used to the more aggressive ways of the suffragettes, were surprised by her frailness and femininity.

4 Her words, too, radiated love and concern. "The first right of every child is to be wanted, to be desired, to be planned with an intensity of love that gives it its title to being," she said. Then she stated seven circumstances under which birth control, in her opinion, must be practiced: Six of her reasons were self-evident for physiological and economic reasons (health of the parents, genetic and financial factors, spacing of children, adolescent marriages), the seventh (practice of birth control for one or two years after marriage so that the couple could "grow together, cement the bonds of attraction, and plan for their children") was novel. In a lighter vein Margaret Sanger proposed a bureau of application for the unborn:

I pictured a married couple coming here for a baby as though for a chambermaid, chauffeur, or gardener. The unborn child took a look at his prospective parents and propounded a few questions such as any employee has the right to ask of his employer.

To his father the unborn child said, "Do you happen to have a health certificate?"

And to the mother, "How are your nerves? What do you know about babies? What kind of a table do you set?"

And to both of them, "What are your plans for bringing me up? Am I to spend my childhood days in factories or mills, or am I to have the opportunities offered by an intelligent, healthy, family life? I am unusually gifted," the baby might add. "Do you know how to develop my talents? What sort of society have you made for the fullest expression of my genius?"

All babies came back to the practical question, "How many children have you already?"

"Eight."

"How much are you earning?"

"Ten dollars a week."

"And living in two rooms, you say? No, thank you. Next please."

As expected, Margaret Sanger was not received everywhere with open arms. Headlines in St. Louis claimed that "1,200 almost in riot over Mrs. Sanger"; she was locked out of a prepaid auditorium in Akron, Ohio, and jailed in Portland, Oregon. But wherever she went she attracted so much attention that the press had to give her front-page coverage. During the three and a half months of her tour she made birth control into one of the most hotly debated topics of the nation.

Her visit to Holland had convinced her that pamphlets and printed literature were not enough. She must establish clinics in which all women—rich or poor—would be helped freely and sympathetically. Brownsville, a "dingy and squalid" village of Brooklyn, was to be her testing ground. A fifty dollar contribution sent by a Los Angeles admirer covered the rent for the first month. Secondhand furniture, an examination table, and gallons of white paint made the two rooms as "hospital looking" as possible.

When everything was ready, Margaret Sanger informed the district attorney of Brooklyn of her intention to dispense contraceptive information. Then she, her sister Ethel, and Fania Mindell, a coworker from Chicago, personally distributed five thousand notices in English, Italian, and Yiddish.

MOTHERS!
Can you afford to have a large family?
Do you want any more children?
If not, why do you have them?
DO NOT KILL, DO NOT TAKE LIFE, BUT PREVENT
Safe, Harmless Information can be obtained of trained Nurses at
46 AMBOY STREET
NEAR PITKIN AVE.—BROOKLYN
Tell Your Friends and Neighbors.   All Mothers Welcome
A registration fee of 10 cents entitles any mother to this information.

On October 16, 1916, the first free birth-control clinic in America opened its doors.

The nurses did not have to wait for customers. From early morning on, the women were standing in line halfway to the corner, "at least one hundred and fifty, some shawled, some hatless, their red hands clasping the cold, chapped, smaller ones of their children."

The little clinic in Brownsville, of course, did not remain undisturbed long. October 26, the tenth day of its existence, it was closed as a public nuisance. Margaret Sanger spent the night in jail, but was released on bail. Later she reopened the clinic only to be jailed again. The women in the neighborhood grieved and the cry of despair of one of them, "Come back, come back and save me," were the last words Mrs. Sanger heard as she was driven off in the police van.

The principal charge brought against Margaret Sanger and her associates was that of violating Section 1142 of the Penal Code, which specifically prohibited the dissemination of birth-control information. Since one of the purposes of the Brownsville clinic

Brownsville, New York, site of America's first birth-control clinic.

had been to test the constitutionality of this paragraph in the courts, Margaret Sanger intended to fight her case through to the highest court of the state. This, she knew, required a lawyer versed in "whereas and whatsoever, and inasmuchases." She thus accepted the free services of Jonah J. Goldstein, a young Jewish lawyer, who in his youth had been infused by the social spirit of Greenwich House and the Henry Street Settlement in New York City.

When the trial opened the courtroom was clogged with Brownsville mothers, their many children in tow. They were hungry because no kosher food was available in the neighborhood, but they stayed. One by one the mothers were called to testify:

"Have you ever seen Mrs. Sanger before?"
"Yess. Yess, I know Mrs. Sanger."
"Where did you see her?"
"At the cleenic."
"Why did you go there?"
"To have her stop the babies."
Then it was the turn of another and another and another:
"How many children have you?"
"Eight and three that didn't live."
"What does your husband earn?"
"Ten dollars a veek—ven he vorks."

That was all Judge Freschi could take that day, and he adjourned the court.

The judge was ready to let Mrs. Sanger off free, pending the appeal, if she promised to refrain from violating Section 1142. But Mrs. Sanger refused to "be good." As she told the court:

I'd like to have it understood by the gentlemen of the Court that the offer of leniency is very kind and I appreciate it very much. With me it is not a question of personal imprisonment or personal disadvantage. I am today and have always been more concerned with changing the law and the sweeping away of the law, regardless of what I have to undergo to have it done.

Thus Margaret Sanger went to the workhouse. Her radiant personality and immense interest in all that was human managed to turn those thirty days into a success. Her fellow prisoners were prostitutes, petty thieves, embezzlers, drug addicts, safecrackers, and other social "dropouts." They, as well as Mrs. Sullivan, the

Margaret Sanger (left) and her sister Ethel Byrnem, in court, in New York City.

matron, became the friends of the unusual prisoner, who within a few days had organized reading and writing classes, for to her surprise she found a high degree of illiteracy among her fellow prisoners.

On March 6, 1917, Margaret Sanger's term was up. As she recalled later:

Through the metal doors I stepped, and the tingling air beat against my face. No other experience in my life has been like that. Gathered in front were my old friends who had frozen through the two hours waiting to celebrate "Margaret's coming out party." They lifted their voices in the *Marseillaise*. Behind them at the upper windows were my new friends, the women with whom I had spent the month, and they too were singing. Something choked me. Something still chokes me whenever I hear that triumphant music and ringing words, "Ye sons of freedom wake to glory!"

During her quiet days in prison Margaret Sanger had decided to change her tactics:

The tempestuous season of agitation—courts and jails and shrieking and thumbing-the-nose—should now end. . . . The next three steps were to be: first, education; then, organization; and finally, legislation. I based my program on the existence in the country of a forceful sentiment which, if co-ordinated, could become powerful enough to change laws. Horses wildly careening around a pasture have as much strength as when harnessed to a plow, but only in the latter case can the strength be measured and turned to some useful purpose.

To fulfill her first aim, education, Margaret Sanger founded the *Birth Control Review,* which, although in continuous financial trouble, was the spearhead of the educational campaign from 1917 to 1921. She also saw to it that the birth-control movement lost its aura of the barricades, and soon it counted among its champions many of the intellectual and social leaders of America.

Mrs. Sanger had always considered birth control mainly a medical problem, and now she actively sought the support of the medical profession. Jonah J. Goldstein had appealed Margaret Sanger's case through the various courts, and on January 8, 1918, Judge Frederick E. Crane of the Court of Appeals, the highest appeals court in the state, rendered the final decision. The judge upheld Margaret Sanger's conviction. By writing a broad interpretation of Section 1142, however, he actually gave her many of the objectives she had been fighting for.

Section 1145 states that physicians can give advice to prevent or cure disease. Until now this had been considered to apply only to syphilis and gonorrhea. By accepting *Webster's Dictionary's* broad definition of disease, "an alteration in the state of the body, or of some of its organs, interrupting or disturbing the performance of the vital functions, and causing or threatening pain or sickness; illness; sickness; disorder," Judge Crane now legally empowered doctors to give married couples birth-control advice.

Though extremely pleased with this decision, Margaret Sanger was not yet satisfied. She wanted women to be able to have birth-control information not only for health reasons but also for economic and social ones. She thus took her fight to Albany and started searching for a legislator to sponsor a bill that would change New York's law.

Margaret Sanger, later in life.

Margaret Sanger had taken up the fight for birth control in 1913; less than a decade later her fame had spread beyond her home state and homeland. Since she lived to be 81 years old, she witnessed more victories than most reformers are lucky enough to see. Her work, however, is still not completed. When Dr. Beasley decided to establish family-planning centers in Louisiana, he too was faced with legal problems. The Catholic Church today is torn by dissent over its stand on the matter, and there is still controversy in state legislatures, Congress and the courts.

But court fights, clinics, and education are only half the battle. Mankind as yet has no perfect contraceptive, and though birth control can easily be considered the world's most pressing health problem, contraceptive technology only recently became an acceptable topic of scientific investigation.

This is perhaps comforting, for in the past when scientists have zeroed in on a problem, they have come up with spectacular solutions in record time. The atom bomb was assembled in half a dozen years, and it took even less time to develop the new strains of wheat and rice that have given the world a short breathing spell before it may be overtaken by famine.

New methods of birth control will, it is to be hoped, be developed over the next dozen years. Both the Pill and the IUD are still in their infancy, and since they are under heavy criticism, they may in the end be only stepping stones in man's quest for the perfect contraceptive. Today's pills, for instance, have been compared by some birth controllers to "sledgehammers used to kill mosquitoes."

Before more selective methods of birth control can be developed, scientists must gain a better understanding of the human reproductive system. Though reproduction and contraceptive research have attained some priority, the topics themselves are far from novel, for man has always wondered how he came to be.

At this point in the history of birth control, we can look back at what we know already and dream about the future, when at long last scientists will present us with a contraceptive that is safe, effective, inexpensive, reversible, easy to use, and acceptable to a diversity of people and cultural groups.

5
The Search
for the Mammalian Egg

From the time they attempted to understand the problem of generation until the question was settled in the nineteenth century, scientists were divided into two schools of thought. The first included those who believed that the womb of Eve, the primordial woman, had contained the seeds of all the human beings who would ever live on earth. The second faction, which was far more powerful since it included such luminaries as Aristotle, Harvey, and Leeuwenhoek, was convinced that the seminal fluid of the male somehow contained the germ from which a new being would grow in its entirety. Since women obviously played a part in the process, it was assumed that they provided something equivalent to soil, or as Aristotle put it, "the wood necessary to build a piece of furniture." The semen of the male, the Greek scientist believed, "played the role of the carpenter who is able to shape the wood to his liking."

Early biologists were hampered by the fact that dissection of human cadavers was prohibited on moral or religious grounds. When this taboo finally eroded during the Italian Renaissance, medical science came into its own.

The foundations of anatomy were laid by Andreas Vesalius, a young man, largely self-taught on corpses stolen from local cemeteries and gallows, who had come to Italy from his native Belgium. When he resigned his chair in Padua at the age of twenty-nine, he had given the world a great medical book, *De Humani Corporis Fabrica,* the first true text of anatomy and one of the most beautiful books ever published.

Vesalius' chair in Padua went to Gabriel Fallopius, whose family name derives from the Italian word *falloppe*—an imperfect silk cocoon.

Gabriel Fallopius

Vesalius had seen the human body as a "fabric" of interwoven parts; Fallopius and others would devote themselves to the examination of the component parts and explore the functions of various organs.

Since the gallows were the chief source of bodies for dissection, female cadavers were scarce. Fallopius nevertheless must have gotten hold of a few, because he left an accurate description of the uterus, the ovaries, the vagina, and the tubes that connect the ovaries and the uterus. Fallopius called them the *uteri tuba,* or trumpets of the uterus, because, as he wrote, "they resemble nothing as much as the bent part of a brass trumpet." The trumpets did not keep their descriptive name for long; shortly after their discoverer's death, in 1562, they began to be referred to as the Fallopian tubes (now also known as oviducts).

The chair of anatomy now went to Fabricius ab Aquapendente, who taught in Padua for more than forty years, making numerous contributions to anatomy and physiology. He also founded modern embryology and wrote the first illustrated text on the subject, which, not surprisingly, deals with the development of chicks.

Fabricius' most illustrious student was not Italian but English. William Harvey arrived in Padua in 1598, and it was there, in the city that Shakespeare called "the nursery of all arts," that he gathered the ideas that formed the basis of his life's work.

Harvey's greatest contribution to science was the discovery of the circulation of the blood. His book on the subject, *De Motu Cordis,* was published in 1628 in Frankfurt, Germany. It was, of course, written in Latin, and like *De Humani Corporis Fabrica,* marks a milestone in medicine.

Harvey, very reluctantly, however, published another book, this one called *De Generatione Animalium.* Its most famous statement is found inscribed on the allegorical illustration of the title page: A bearded Jupiter is holding a cornucopia-type egg, out of which spills forth an assortment of fantastic and realistic creatures. On the egg it says *Ex ova omnia* or "everything comes from the egg."

Harvey had started his embryological studies in the classical manner by incubating hens' eggs in his chambers at Oxford. As the physician and personal friend of King Charles I, who took a lively interest in science, Harvey also had the opportunity to study deer.

The king had granted Harvey permission to perform autopsies on the animals shot during royal hunting expeditions. Since

Harvey wanted to study the very young embryo, he availed himself of this privilege in the fall—during and shortly after the deer's mating season. Harvey, like Aristotle, believed that the embryo was generated from the combination of the "substance" (the menstrual blood of the female) and the "spirit" emitted by the seminal fluid. These, according to Harvey's speculations, would combine into a blood-tinged mixture that he expected to find in the uterus.

To his surprise and dismay, however, he found that the uteri of the royal does were empty! During the first two weeks after mating, "all the eyes could see were a soft swollen lining and some filamentous membranes that resembled nothing as much as spider webs."

At first Harvey thought that in that particular year the deer had not mated, as they usually did, between mid-September and mid-October. This explanation was dispelled when the king let him capture and keep a number of presumably pregnant does. Half of

William Harvey (center) dissecting a doe in front of his friend and patron, King Charles I of England.

these were killed soon after capture and had the now familiar "empty" womb, whereas the "controls" produced their fawns on schedule the following spring.

To Harvey, the appearance of the young embryo thus remained a mystery. Since he could not find any embryonic material, he concluded that the male semen never actually reached the uterus but merely sent up a spirit, which caused the spidery material to secrete an egg, much as "the brain can form an idea" or "a painter can paint a landscape from memory."

Harvey must not have been very happy with the conclusions he had reached, however, for he did not publish *De Generatione Animalium.* It was only reluctantly that he gave the manuscript to a friend, who saw to its publication in 1651. Its erroneous conclusions, coupled with the fame of its author, were perhaps one of the reasons why mammalian embryology remained a relatively unstudied subject.

Harvey had had to examine the does with the naked eye. Now the vision of biologists was expanded with microscopes. One of the first to use these was Anton van Leeuwenhoek. Born in Delft in 1632, he had little formal education and was a draper by trade. Nobody knows when he started to fashion his unparalleled "glasses" and wander with them through nature, examining raindrops, pus, blood, and other things, finding wherever he looked a teeming world of *animalculae,* or "little animals."

For a long time he kept what he saw to himself, but science as we know it today came into being during the seventeenth century. The Royal Society of London had just been founded, and a friend persuaded Leeuwenhoek to write to this august assembly. In his first letter to the organization Leeuwenhoek explained why he had often declined to publish his discoveries:

First, I have no style or pen wherewith to express my thoughts properly; secondly, because I have not been brought up to language or art [all his letters were in his native tongue], but only to business; and in the third place because I do not gladly suffer contradiction or censure from others. This resolve of mine, however, I have now set aside, at the entreaty of Dr. Regnerus de Graaf; and I gave him a memoir on what I have noticed about the mould, the sting and sundry limbs of the bee, and also about the sting of the louse. . . .

Anton van Leeuwenhoek

Both Leeuwenhoek and the Royal Society must have found the exchange mutually satisfactory, and for the next fifty years he faithfully wrote letters to London, his discoveries being so numerous as "to fill four pretty large volumes in Quarto." In the end he willed to the society "those Instruments he so long us'd [and] so much improv'd."

In 1674 Leeuwenhoek and his student Hamen discovered spermatozoa, the "little animals of the male seminal fluid." To Leeuwenhoek they seemed the final proof of the Aristotelian view that it is the male who provides the female with a "miniature man" from which an entire being starts to unfold. In the centuries to come, members of this scientific faction were called the "spermatists," as opposed to the "ovists," whose first and most important proponent also lived in Holland.

He was the same Regnier de Graaf who had introduced Leeuwenhoek to the Royal Society. Unlike his friend, he was professionally trained. He had studied at the University of Leyden, which is probably the first educational institution to be built with taxpayers' money. It had been a gift of King William the Silent, who wanted to reward the town for resisting, in 1564, the armies sent by Philip II of Spain. William had given the burghers the choice of ten tax-free years or the establishment of a university. They had opted for education, and soon the reputation of Leyden's medical school spread across Europe. It was visited not only by the famous scientists of the day but also by Holland's artists. Rembrandt was a frequent guest, and his painting, *The Anatomy Lesson,* as well as numerous sketches, bear witness to the time he spent there.

De Graaf studied at Leyden when it had already attained the height of its fame. Not content merely to minister to the ill, he was also active in research. He was the first to investigate the digestive juices produced by the pancreatic and salivary glands, and today he is often considered to be "the father of biochemistry." De Graaf also investigated the reproductive process.

The fertilized hen egg and the developing chick embryo, which for good reasons had always been the favorite subject of the embryologists, had already been scrutinized by Marcello Malpighi with a microscope. Malpighi was a contemporary of De Graaf and Leeuwenhoek, and also a correspondent of the Royal Society in London. His work prompted Regnier De Graaf to take another look at the reproductive organs of women and other mammals. He was struck at once by the resemblance of the mammalian ovaries to those found in birds. He also noticed on the surface of these ovaries small blisterlike formations. De Graaf believed these follicles to be the mammalian egg. Commenting on the fact that they were unprotected he wrote:

It is of no importance that the ova of women are not, like those of fowls, enveloped in a hard shell, for the latter are incubated outside the body in order to hatch the chickens, but the former remain within the female body during the development, and are protected as thoroughly from all injuries by the uterus as by a shell."

Like Harvey, De Graaf also attempted to discover the early embryo. He was luckier in his choice of experimental animals and worked with rabbits, then as now symbols of unlimited fertility. After observing the mating of buck and doe, he killed the female after longer and longer intervals and examined their reproductive

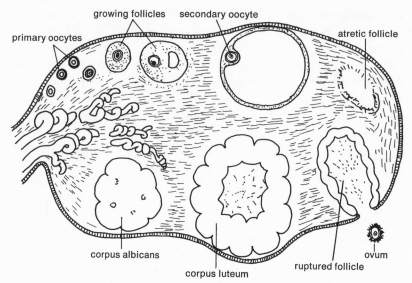

growing follicles · secondary oocyte

primary oocytes

atretic follicle

corpus albicans

corpus luteum

ruptured follicle

ovum

Different events take place in the ovary during a cycle. In reality they take place one at a time in an ovary, but are shown here, for convenience, in successive stages.

organs. He did not use a microscope, and for the first two days saw nothing worth noting. On the third day he found small spheres in the ovarian tubes, and a day later he saw similar ones, only slightly bigger, in the uterus itself. De Graaf was most surprised that these spheres were much smaller than the ovarian follicles that he considered to be the entire ova.

De Graaf published his work on ovaries in 1672. Soon thereafter it was attacked by two fellow scientists who claimed priority. It is known that De Graaf was most distressed by the dispute, and perhaps it contributed to his early death. He died at the age of thirty-two, but his name lives on in the "Graafian follicles," the small fluid-filled blisters he had noted on the surface of the ovaries. These, it turned out, were not the true mammalian egg after all, and one hundred sixty years were to pass until De Graaf's quest was brought to a successful conclusion by Karl Ernst von Baer.

Von Baer was born in 1792, in a region of Russia that is now part of Estonia. He studied medicine in Eastern Europe, and in order to please his parents, who wanted him to practice medicine, he went to Vienna to perfect his clinical skills. But von Baer was discouraged by the unscientific spirit of the Viennese clinics and hospitals where, at the time, "everything was left to nature." When two of his friends told him that things were better at the University of Würzburg in southern Germany, he went there. In addition to his own belongings he took two samples of dried moss, entrusted to him by his two colleagues. They were to serve as his introduction to J. Döllinger, a professor of anatomy and an inspiring teacher whose lectures von Baer was advised to attend.

Professor Döllinger did not lecture that term, but he took a liking to the eager young messenger and invited him to work in his laboratory. "Why lectures?" he said. "Come back with any old creature so that we can dismember it together."

Karl Ernst von Baer

In his haste, von Baer could only find a leech, which he bought from a local apothecary, and it was perhaps the smallness of this animal that led him to examine other small objects. Aside from dissecting leeches, von Baer also learned much about the embryology of the chick, a subject to which his professor devoted a major part of his scientific life.

His experiences in Würzburg determined von Baer's career. He never entered the practice of medicine, but devoted himself to teaching and research. Success came early when, at age thirty-three, he decided to investigate the early embryological development of dogs. Like Harvey and De Graaf before him, he planned to sacrifice, and examine, female dogs at regular intervals of one, two, and three and of twelve and twenty-four days after mating. However, he introduced a seemingly minor modification in technique, which proved decisive in his quest.

Instead of looking at the dog with the one-day-old embryo first, he planned his experiments so that he first examined the dog that

THE MATURE OVUM TRAVELS FROM THE OVARY TO THE UTERUS

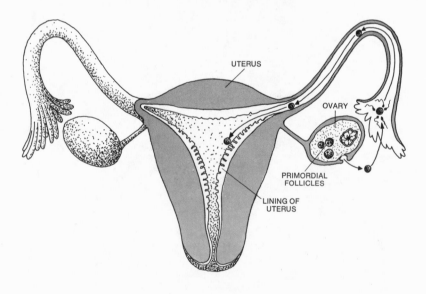

Fertilization takes place in the Fallopian tubes. The fertilized ovum already starts dividing (cleaving) during its trip through the tubes, and the resulting blastocyte is implated (nidates) approximately one week after ovulation.

carried the twenty-four-day-old embryo, then that with the twelve-day-old embryo, gradually working his way backward to the time the "egg" had not yet been fertilized. Awareness of the appearance of a more advanced development facilitated his recognition of the preceding stage. In this manner von Baer found in the uterus the spherical blastocysts (primitive fertilized ova) that De Graaf had seen on the fourth day after conception. In another dog he saw similar organisms in the Fallopian tubes themselves, obviously on their way down to the uterus. Von Baer later recalled:

The next step was to learn the state of the ova in the ovary, for it is very clear that such minute eggs cannot be the Graafian follicles themselves, expelled from the ovary, nor does it seem likely that such solid corpuscles as we find the tubal ova to be, are formed by coagulation of the follicular fluid. Examination of the ovaries before making any incision I saw plainly,

Human spermatozoon with "preformed man" (homunculus) after Hartsoeker (1772).

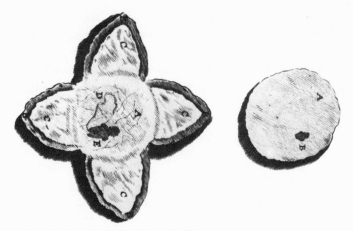

a. Ovum three to four days after it reached uterus.
b. Human ovum two weeks after conception. Note placenta, umbilical cord and
   homunculus.

in almost every follicle, a yellowish-white point; and by pressing with a probe it appeared clear that it was not in any way attached to the wall of the follicle, but floated freely in the fluid. Led by curiosity rather than by any thought that I had seen the ovules in the ovaries through all the layers of the graafian follicles, I opened one of the follicles and took the minute object on the point of my knife, finding that I could see it very distinctly and that it was surrounded by mucus. When I placed it under the microscope I was utterly astonished, for I saw an ovule just as I had already seen them in the tubes, and so clearly that a blind man could hardly deny it. It is truly wonderful and surprising to be able to demonstrate to the eye, by so simple a procedure, a thing which has been sought so persistently and discussed *ad nauseam* in every textbook of physiology, as insoluble.

Von Baer had carried out the final phase of his experiment on May 1, 1827, a century and a half after De Graaf had experimented with rabbits and two hundred years after Harvey had been given permission to examine the does of the royal hunting preserve near Hampton Court.

Embryology, and, as a matter of fact, all of biology, was to be put on a firm footing eleven years later, in 1838, when two German scientists, M. J. Schleiden and Theodor Schwann, stated that all living matter consists of cells. A few years later Schwann speculated that the mammalian ovum is a single cell. This was confirmed in 1861 by another German scientist, Karl Gegenbaur, whose teacher, Albert von Kölliker, had traced the development of spermatozoa in the testes and shown that they too consist of single cells.

When it was finally demonstrated that during fertilization one egg cell and one sperm cell—the largest and the smallest cells of the human organism—fuse into a single cell, the ancient war of the spermatists and ovists was settled in a manner that proved both factions had been wrong.

6
Physiology
Comes of Age

The anatomists and microscopists could only discover part of the story of human reproduction. Physiology had to come of age before the entire process could be understood more completely.

It is self-evident that the overall development of any living creature proceeds according to a rigid timetable. For man it takes nine months from conception to birth, another nine, approximately, for the child to grow teeth, and a whole eighteen years for it to become full-grown.

It is, however, not only overall development that unfolds according to a predetermined manner. Life processes are regulated by a series of biological clocks that tick at different rates for different species. Man sleeps about eight hours a day; bears, turtles, and frogs hibernate; cats catnap; birds migrate; and whereas some creatures have to eat almost constantly, others fast for long periods of time.

Most biological cycles are so intimately woven into the pattern of everyday life that one is barely aware of their existence. An exception is the cycle associated with reproduction. For many

48

animals mating time is tied to the calendar. The does that Harvey investigated so long ago in England mated only between September 15 and October 15, as they still do in that part of the world. The fawns are thus born in spring, when leaves and young branches are at their most plentiful.

In May of each year salmon travel across oceans, rivers, and waterfalls in order to spawn at the head of the same stream their parents did. In spring too, the birds come back to lay their eggs in nests they may have built the previous year, and though domestic animals long ago ceased to fend for themselves, spring is the time that barnyards, stables, and pastures are full of chicks, lambs, foals, and kittens.

Man's reproductive life is not tied to the calendar, yet the rhythmical pattern of a woman's menstrual cycle is a clear indication that it is regulated by a biological clock, as is puberty itself. It had always been assumed that such "clocks," as well as strong emotions, were regulated by some mysterious, powerful substances; therefore, primitive man ate the entrails of brave animals to give himself courage. Later on, one school of doctors, the organotherapists, prescribed various organ extracts and powders to cure some specific diseases, but it was not until almost our own times that scientists discovered the true nature of these powerful "spirits."

Practice often precedes knowledge by hundreds and even thousands of years. Long before anybody knew why it worked, farmers were castrating male animals so as to alter their characteristics. Removal of the sex glands turned aggressive cockerels into tender capons and fierce bulls into docile steers.

Oriental potentates availed themselves of this same minor "surgical intervention" to produce impotent, fat eunuchs to guard their harems, and the church used to castrate a number of young boys so that they could continue to sing soprano parts in the all-male choirs.

For us, who have inherited so much knowledge, it is difficult to conceive that all the great minds of the past failed to conclude from these facts that the testes must produce a chemical substance essential to manhood. The crucial experiment demonstrating its presence was finally done in 1848, but even then the world was not ready to accept its meaning, and the experimenter himself chose to ignore this, his most important work.

49

He was Arnold Adolph Berthold—a professor of zoology at Germany's famous Göttingen University. Though the professor had a well-equipped laboratory on campus, he chose to carry out his most memorable research in the privacy of his own backyard, where he kept a few chickens.

He took four cockerels and surgically removed their testicles. Two of the castrated cocks—or capons—were allowed to return to the chicken run; the other two underwent a second operation. The professor took one of their testicles and implanted it in their abdominal cavity. Then they too were allowed to rejoin the flock.

As time went on there was a great difference between the two pairs of birds. The two that had simply been castrated lost all their male characteristics. Their combs drooped and became discolored; they became fat and lazy and paid no attention whatsoever to the hens of the barnyard.

The other two—those that had a single testicle, but in the wrong place—seemed none the worse for the experience. They strutted and crowed, fought with their rivals, and mounted the hens.

Berthold now sacrificed these two roosters and found that a network of capillaries had developed between the implanted testicles and the wall of the abdomen. Since no nerve tissue had

Left: a castrated rooster or capon has a small undeveloped comb and wattles.
Right: a capon which has received daily injections of male hormones.

regenerated, Berthold concluded that "the testes act upon the blood and the blood acts correspondingly upon the entire organism."

The German professor published his findings in the *Archives of Anatomy, Physiology and Medical Science* in 1848, then he returned to more conventional research, apparently forgetting about his experiment. So did the world—for a while at least. His paper, simply entitled "Transplantation of Testicles," gathered dust on library shelves, to be resurrected only in 1910, by which time others had painfully proven again what he had demonstrated so simply and brilliantly.

It often happens in science that suddenly a subject that has remained dormant for years, even centuries, starts to blossom. Major discoveries are made, often simultaneously, in different laboratories, as if the investigators were endowed with extrasensory perception. So it was with physiology during the second half of the nineteenth century.

The central figure in this story was a Frenchman, Claude Bernard. He was born in 1813. In his native town he had worked as an assistant in the local pharmacy. When his chores permitted, he had put pen to paper, and when he was almost thirty he went to Paris to make his mark as a dramatist. He showed his masterpiece—*Arthur de Bretagne*—to the leading drama critic Saint-Marc Girardin. It is not known what this expert thought of the play, but in any case he counseled Bernard to study medicine while waiting for literary fame. Bernard did, and in due time was invited to lecture at the Collège de France, where he opened his lecture with the remark: "Scientific medicine, which it ought to be my duty to teach, does not exist." In less than two decades, largely because of his efforts, a special chair of experimental medicine was created at the Sorbonne University in Paris.

Bernard's contributions to physiology are many. He started out by investigating the pancreatic juice, a subject that had been taken up and abandoned by Regnier de Graaf two hundred years earlier. Then Bernard went on to his most important work, the manner in which sugar is metabolized (changed and utilized) in the liver. But Bernard is perhaps best remembered for stating that the body functions as a single, separate entity whose operation depends on an exact balance and correct interplay of all "body fluids." He likened the fluids of the body to an "internal environment" that must remain constant at all costs and is responsible for the fact that land creatures can survive away from the external aquatic environment from which all life emerged.

Bernard's successors, as well as the scientists of today, have continued to search for the mechanisms that keep this internal environment constant. The experiment that put all these investigators on the right track was performed in 1902 by two Englishmen, William Maddock Bayliss and Ernest Henry Starling, who identified one of the chemical messengers involved in digestion. They called the substance secretin—because it causes the pancreas to "secrete" pancreatic juice at the precise moment it is needed.

Bayliss and Starling realized that secretin was only one of many chemical messengers. They called this group of substances "hormones," from the Greek verb *hormaein,* "to excite" or "put in motion." Hormones are manufactured in the body by the endocrine, or ductless, glands—so called because they pour their products directly into the blood stream—as well as by individual cells that have no recognizable glandular structure.

The discovery of secretin opened a whole new field of research. Scientists turned with renewed vigor to the various organs and glands and discovered that they manufacture a host of chemical messengers. (The adrenal glands alone put out more than forty-five different ones!) These hormones were found to regulate growth, sugar utilization, blood pressure, salt balance, heart rate, blood flow, and many other long- and short-term processes, and at first scientists thought that a complete understanding of how the body operates was within reach. Matters were, however, far from simple, for it turned out that most processes were controlled by several hormones working in seesaw fashion.

This seemed particularly true of the sex hormones. Berthold had shown that the testes manufacture a chemical factor that can maintain an animal's male characteristics even when the glands themselves are transplanted into another part of the body. The testicles themselves, however, are under the control of the small pituitary gland, nestled at the base of the brain and connected with the hypothalamus by a narrow stalk. In man the pituitary gland measures about half an inch in diameter at its widest; nevertheless, it consists of several distinct parts.

The interrelationship of the pituitary and the sex glands has been known for some time. Removal of the pituitary causes symptoms of castration that resemble those observed when the primary sex glands are removed in both men and women. Normal function is re-established when the animal is supplied with pituitary extracts or receives a graft of pituitary tissue.

Immature animals that have been deprived of their pituitaries fail to mature sexually. (Since the pituitary also manufactures the growth hormone, overall growth comes to a halt.) Again, as in all typical hormone-deprivation experiments, growth and sexual maturation are resumed when the animal is supplied with pituitary grafts or extracts.

Detailed research has shown that the anterior lobe of the pituitary manufactures two sex hormones, which are of paramount importance to reproduction. Together they are referred to as the "gonadotropic hormones." ("Tropic," from the Greek *tropos,* to turn or stimulate, indicates what organ or gland a hormone is acting on. The gonadotropic hormones "stimulate the gonads." The latter word is the collective name of the testicles and ovaries.) One gonadotropin is called the "follicle-stimulating hormone," or FSH for short, because when it was discovered its only function seemed to be to trigger the ripening of the mammalian egg in its follicle. Later it was shown that pituitary control of sex function is much more complex. At puberty FSH stimulates the development of both testes and ovaries, and in adulthood it is essential to maintain normal sex function in both males and females.

The second gonadotropin goes by two names. In the female it is called the "lutenizing hormone," or LH, because its chief function is to promote the development of the corpus luteum, the yellow body that develops in the ovarian follicle after it has released the egg. In the male it is called the "interstitial cell-stimulating hormone," or ICSH. Its name derives from the fact that it stimulates the secretion of the male sex hormone by the interstitial cells (the cells that lie in-between the sex cells of the testes). Like FSH, it contributes to both the development and maintenance of the entire male reproductive apparatus. Since subsequent research proved LH and ICSH to be one and the same, today the hormone usually goes by its "female" name.

Even though they are essential for sexual development and function, the gonadotropins are not the primary sex hormones. In 1896, half a century after Berthold's "forgotten" experiment, the

Viennese gynecologist Emil Knauer proved that the ovaries, which sometimes have been called the female testes, secrete a substance responsible for secondary female sexual characteristics. To prove the existence of this substance, Knauer resorted to almost exactly the same procedure Berthold had used. Ovaries were removed from adult guinea pigs, and the animals showed typical signs of castration, which vanished when Knauer reimplanted parts of the ovaries. A few years later another Viennese scientist, Josef Halban, showed that the uteri of infantile guinea pigs would grow to adult size when he grafted bits of ovaries under their skin.

Berthold, Knauer, and other early hormone hunters had contented themselves with demonstrating that hormones were indeed manufactured by the gonads. The next generation of scientists was bent on isolating and identifying these principles. They were hampered by the fact that the body manufactures these key substances in minute amounts only.

In spite of dedication, and an enormous number of ovaries, those attempting to isolate the female sex hormone could do little more than repeatedly prove its existence. In 1927 a discovery in a related field came to their rescue. Drs. Selmar Aschheim and Bernhard Zondek discovered that when a sexually immature laboratory mouse is injected with urine of a pregnant woman, the mouse will go into heat (estrus) within twenty-four hours. The urine of nonpregnant women does not cause such a reaction. This procedure, now called the Aschheim-Zondek test, was welcomed by the medical profession because it was a reliable means of diagnosing pregnancy weeks before a woman showed any obvious physical changes.

The news created excitement in hormone research. By the 1920's research had ceased to be a lonely occupation pursued by a few isolated scientists. To those involved, it became a very serious competition in which it mattered terribly who got there first.

As soon as the German doctors published their test, hormone hunters realized that the changes in the immature mice could only be caused by hormones whose manufacture, during pregnancy, was stepped up to such an extent that the excess spilled over into the urine. Consequently, scientists working in Swiss, German, American, and Dutch laboratories "dropped" their ovaries and began to process enormous quantities of pregnancy urine.

The switch proved profitable. Within two years the American team, headed by Drs. Edgar Allen and Edward Doisy of Washington University in St. Louis, were able to announce that they had isolated a few grains of the elusive female sex hormone. They called their find "estrone," because it caused estrus in mice. Victory by the American team came in the nick of time. A bare two months later a German group also reached the goal.

Later it was shown that several closely related substances cause an estrus-type reaction. Today these are collectively referred to as estrogens.

ESTRADIOL   **ESTRONE**

Identification and isolation of the estrogens nevertheless left many questions unanswered, and the feeling that not one but two hormones play a major role in female reproduction increased. Unlike the testes of the male, which from puberty manufacture a steady stream of sperm cells, the ovaries of the female work like a precise timepiece.

From animal experiments scientists knew that the reproductive cycle of the female is associated with the maturation of egg cells that are released from the ovaries at regular intervals: once a year for does and other creatures whose life is intimately linked to the seasons, two to three times a year for dogs, once every four weeks for women, once every three weeks for sows, once every four to five days for rats. Each egg matures inside a little sac, the ovarian follicle. During the maturation process the ovum and the follicle move toward the outer edge of the ovary. At ovulation the follicle ruptures, releasing the egg, which starts on its way down the oviducts. Its place in the now-empty follicle is rapidly taken up by the corpus luteum.

Since it was first described by Regnier de Graaf in 1672, the role of the corpus luteum had so completely mystified those interested that in 1909 a French student amused himself by listing twenty-five different incorrect speculations about its function. Actually he was slightly behind the times, because in 1898 Louis Auguste Prenant had suggested that the corpus luteum might be a gland of internal secretion, producing some sort of hormone for the benefit of the egg with which it is associated, and in 1907 Leo Loeb showed that it is absolutely necessary to maintain the fertilized egg in the uterus.

It was thus quite natural that those scientists who believed in the existence of a second female sex hormone concentrated their efforts on the corpus luteum. As in the case of the estrogens the hunt for this second hormone was pursued by several laboratories. Again the hormone was isolated, almost simultaneously, in Europe and in America. The honor of naming it fell to the first to get there: George Washington Corner and Willard M. Allen of the University of Rochester. The hormone was called "progesterone" because it favored gestation.

Its identification, together with an understanding of how the hormones released by the pituitary operate, finally explained the nature of the female reproductive cycle.

Two sex hormones (gonadotropins), made by the pituitary, play a

PROGESTERONE   TESTOSTERONE

major role in the regulation of the menstrual cycle: the follicle stimulating hormone, FSH, and the lutenizing hormone, LH. As its name implies, FSH stimulates the ovaries to ripen one or several follicles. It also initiates estrogen production. Once the egg (or eggs) is ripe inside the follicle, it is released, enters the fallopian tube, and descends toward the uterus. In the meantime the second gonadotropic hormone, LH, directs the formation of the corpus luteum, which starts to manufacture progesterone. The first task of progesterone is to prepare the uterus for nidation, a lovely term derived from the French word *nid,* or "nest." The mammalian equivalent of the nest is the endometrium, a soft lining of the uterus that will shelter and nourish the fetus during the months of pregnancy.

Often, however, there is no fertilization, and the body has no use for the soft nest the uterus has prepared or for a large amount of progesterone. Being superfluous, the corpus luteum withers and dies. Without its support, the uterus sheds its now useless lining during menstruation.

Matters are entirely different if the egg is fertilized. The corpus luteum continues to grow and produce progesterone, as does the placenta. The high level of progesterone informs the pituitary gland that since the organism has no use for additional ripened follicles, it should cut down on follicle-stimulating hormone production. Also, since progesterone production remains high, the uterus does not shed its lining, and there is no menstruation during pregnancy. (See chart page 68.)

Though the presence of the male hormone had been demonstrated half a century before its female counterpart, it was, in the end, to be isolated later. At the time of the hunt for the male hormone, scientists in America and in Germany regularly exceeded their research budgets buying up enormous quantities of testicles from slaughterhouses. From these they hoped to extract the male hormone. Progress was slow but steady, and in the late 1920's scientists were zeroing in on the hormone. Then came the Aschheim-Zondek test, and with it the discovery that urine also contained considerable amounts of the male hormone. The search for the hormone shifted from testicles to urine, and in 1931 Adolph Butenandt, the German scientist who had lost the race for the female hormone by two months, announced that he had isolated a

THE FOUR HORMONES OF THE MENSTRUAL CYCLE

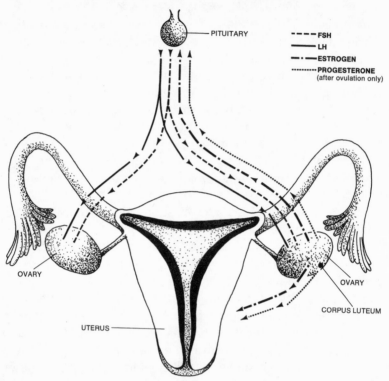

Hormones usually work seesaw fashion. The first hormone of the menstrual cycle is the follicle stimulating hormone (FSH) which stimulates a single primordial follicle. The developing follicle also emits estrogen. By that time the pituitary emits the lutenizing hormone (LH) which initiates the development of corpus luteum (CL) after a mature egg leaves the ovary. CL emits progesterone. Both estrogen and progesterone "tell" pituitary to cut down production of FSH and LH.

likely candidate. It was called "androsterone"—from the Greek word *andros,* man. Closer investigation proved that androsterone was only a close relative of the true male hormone, testosterone.

The hunt for hormones had never been a search made for knowledge's sake only. There always was great hope that once isolated they would prove invaluable from a medical point of view. This was spectacularly proven in 1922 when two Canadians, Frederick Banting and Charles Best, showed that doomed diabetics could lead near-normal lives when supplied daily with a small amount of insulin. Banting and Best had obtained the sugar-regulating hormone from cattle, and, as in many other cases, the animal version of the hormone was similar enough to that of man so that it could be used as a substitute.

Now that they had finally been identified, scientists also hoped to put the sex hormones to good use. They felt confident that these chemicals could correct infertility, impotence, menstrual abnormalities, and, most important perhaps, help habitual aborters carry their babies to term.

There was only one hitch to this. Except for insulin, hormones were frightfully expensive. Progesterone, for example, retailed for $40,000 a pound!

The main reason for the high cost is that hormones, unlike vitamins, fats, or sugars, are not stored in the animal body. Furthermore, since they are so potent, they are never present in large enough amounts to make extraction from animal tissue profitable. The obvious alternative to extraction of ready-made hormones was their preparation from scratch (synthesis). In the 1930's this was a tall order, especially since the sex hormones turned out to be very complicated. All contained a steroid nucleus, which then seemed impossible to prepare in the laboratory.

At the time scientists were struggling with these, then insurmountable technical problems, they were joined by one of the most talented, temperamental, and unpredictable organic chemists of our era.

Russell Marker was born in Hagerstown, Maryland, in 1902, the Year One of hormone history, when Bayliss and Starling had identified secretin. As a child Marker was already strange, lonely, and difficult to get along with. His favorite haunt in his hometown was the public library, and by the time he left for the University of Maryland he had read and reread its small reserve of technical books. In college Marker majored in organic chemistry. He received his bachelor's degree at age twenty-one and stayed on to obtain a doctorate.

He rapidly became a wizard at isolating, identifying, synthesizing, and modifying complex organic molecules, and his doctoral research was completed within two years. Then one day, nobody knows why, he decided he had had enough of the University of Maryland and he left without his degree.

In 1928, after a stint with the Navy and private industry, he

59

showed up at the Rockefeller Institute in New York City, then the mecca of biological research. His unusual talent for synthesizing complex molecules was recognized by Dr. P. A. Levene, and Marker was hired.

For a while he seemed extremely happy at Rockefeller, working at breakneck speed in his corner of the laboratory. Except for playing chess, he kept to himself. He was difficult to work with, but his scientific reputation grew, and within a period of six years he co-authored twenty-six scientific papers dealing with the structure and preparation of organic compounds. His could have been an enviable career at one of the world's most respected research institutions, but Marker was incapable of conventional stability. In 1934, for no apparent reason, he left Rockefeller Institute as he had the University of Maryland.

He had no trouble finding another job. Pennsylvania State College was eager to make him Professor of Organic Chemistry, and Parke-Davis, a pharmaceutical firm in nearby Detroit, was overjoyed to have him as a consultant, since they wanted to capture a large corner of the lucrative hormone market. By that time Marker had become interested in steroids, whose plentiful supply was of such crucial importance to the sex-hormone hunters.

Steroids are a widely distributed family of compounds. They resemble one another by having an identical nucleus of eighteen carbon atoms. They differ from one another with respect to what is attached to this basic nucleus.

CHOLESTEROL

60

The effortless way in which the body converts cholesterol into whatever other steroid substance is needed cannot easily be duplicated in the laboratory, and in the 1930's hormone manufacturers continued to extract prefabricated hormones from animal tissue. Attempts were being made at preparing steroid hormones from materials with a high cholesterol content such as sheep's wool fat, ox bile, or cow spinal chords, but the yields were low and manufacturing costs were high.

Hormones and hormonelike chemicals are, however, not restricted to the animal world. They also control key processes in plants, and in his search for a cheaper raw material for the hormone industry it occurred to Russell Marker that it might be profitable to investigate the plant world. Steroid hormones, he speculated, could perhaps be made from sapogenins, a family of compounds that also contained the by now familiar steroid structure.

Of all the sapogenins, diosgenin, isolated in 1936 by two Japanese scientists, seemed the most promising.

DIOSGENIN

Within a matter of months Marker had succeeded in determining the exact structure of some sapogenins. By means of an efficient five-stage process sapogenins were turned into progesterone. Some more chemical wizardry and progesterone became testosterone.

Marker now set out to find a plant with a high sapogenin content. The roots of members of the lily family, including the yucca, agave, and true yam, were a possibility. Such species are common in Mexico, and during the summer vacation of 1940 Marker and seventeen American and Mexican botanists combed the South-

61

west and Mexico for sapogenin-secreting plants. More than one hundred thousand pounds of roots and other plant products, representing four hundred different species, were shipped to the far-off Pennsylvania State College, where Marker and his students proceeded to analyze their sapogenin content.

It was a long and tedious task. Some roots contained no sapogenins, others contained a trace, but several yielded a large amount. Gradually the search narrowed down to the roots of the Dioscorea plant—or *cabeza de negro* as it is called by the Mexicans—a wild yam growing in the desolate regions of southern Mexico.

Marker was jubilant. He knew that the end of the steroid-hormone famine was in sight. Parke-Davis was less enthusiastic. The project seemed a wild gamble. There was no trained labor force in the Mexican mountains. The cost of shipping the roots to the United States seemed prohibitive. Mexican politics were in a state of turmoil, and foreign investments were a liability. Why not base such a large-scale operation on a plant native to the United States? Soybeans offered some hope.

Marker, a man not given to arguing, spent two years trying to convince Parke-Davis. Then, in 1944, he packed his gear, walked out of the Pennsylvania State College in the middle of the term, and went to Mexico City. There he established a crude laboratory in an unused pottery shed, and set out for the mountains of southern Mexico armed with a machete, a mule, and dozens of burlap bags.

A few months later he appeared in the offices of the Laboratories Hermona in Mexico City, carrying two big glass jars filled with a white crystalline powder: over four pounds of pure progesterone, which, at the current market price, was worth about $160,000!

Dr. Frederick Lehmann, one of the two directors of the Laboratories Hermona, could hardly believe his eyes. If the powder indeed was progesterone—and it was—the man who stood before him was worth a fortune.

Within a couple of days Lehmann, his partner, Emeric Somlo, and Marker had formed a new firm, Syntex Sociédad Anonima, which proceeded to supply the world with progesterone at prices that gradually dropped from astronomical heights. The world price of progesterone, and that of the other sex hormones, had been broken.

Babasco plant harvested by Mexican laborer.

Amicable, long-lasting relationships with others were impossible for Marker. Within a year he quarreled with Lehmann and Somlo, sold them his share of the enterprise, and started to manufacture hormones in a small plant of his own.

With no written records of Marker's procedures and a completely unskilled staff of Mexican workers, Syntex was in trouble. A Hungarian-born organic chemist, George Rosenkranz, came to the rescue of the desperate directors. He quickly succeeded in reinventing Marker's process, and the world continued to be supplied with progesterone.

After his break with Syntex, Marker became even more of a recluse. For a while he continued to do the only thing that seemed to have given his restless soul some satisfaction: scientific research.

Sex hormones were not the only steroid compounds doctors were clamoring for. Cortisone, a steroid compound synthesized by Merck and Co., had "miraculously" restored crippled, bedridden arthritic patients to apparent health. Manufacture of cortisone was extremely costly, and treatment was restricted to a very few.

Again, as in the case of the sex hormones, Marker turned to sapogenins abundantly found in Mexican yams. After eight years of research he succeeded in making cortisone from botogenin, a constituent of a tropical yam often used as a food material in Latin America.

Marker announced this manufacturing process in August, 1949. Several years later he disappeared. From time to time, people claim to have seen him in Mexico City, in small Indian villages, or elsewhere. None of these rumors have been substantiated, and for all intents and purposes he is lost to the world.

The industry he founded single-handedly, however, flourishes. It has supplemented the meager livelihood of the Mexican Indians who gather the roots of the barbasco plant—which has an even higher diosgenin content than the cabeza de negro—in "off-season" when they are not harvesting coffee, beans, bananas, oranges, or sugar cane. It has brought wealth to several big pharmaceutical firms, who have built major production plants in Mexico. Most important, sex hormones were indeed found to be able to correct many hormone-deficiency diseases. Before long, however, they were making even more news in a closely related field: birth control.

7

"I Invented the Pill Because of a Woman"

—Gregory Pincus

Questions in science are like wishes. As soon as one is answered, another comes to the forefront. So it was with the long search for the mammalian egg.

Von Baer had finally seen it in 1823, but even today the understanding of the reproductive system is far from complete. Scientists still do not know why, once a month, women mature a single one of their five million eggs (or at most a very few, if they are one of those rare creatures who have multiplets), what triggers the actual rupture of the follicle, or how the oviduct monitors two-way traffic: strictly ascending for the sperm, strictly descending for the ovum.

It is thus not surprising that scientists continue to be fascinated by some specific aspects of the reproductive process. One such man was Gregory Pincus. He could spend hours watching a small ovum under the microscope without ever becoming bored, and his colleagues knew that although he was one of the world's leading hormone experts and the director of the Worcester Foundation for Experimental Biology Research, the mammalian egg was his first love.

Gregory Pincus

As he recalled shortly before his death:

For more than twenty years I studied everything to do with the mechanism of ovulation, fecundation and gestation in mammals. When one studies mammals, one is quickly led to take an interest in the highest mammal of all, human beings.

My research into sterility and fertility enabled me to make a close study of the mechanisms of ovulation and fecundation and of all the stages through which the fertilized ovule passes in the female tube until it becomes planted in the uterus.

I then discovered that two organs, the hypothalamus and the hypophysis [also called pituitary], controlled by priority the operations preceding ovulation and prepared for it. I asked myself whether it might not be possible to block ovulation by imitating, by artificial means, the processes of nature. This was the question I put to myself gratuitously, merely from the curiosity of a research worker. But one day I was asked to pass from simple curiosity to a practical application. That is when I was harnessed to the task of perfecting the pill. It was 1950.

It will come as no great surprise that the person who recruited him to the cause of contraception was Margaret Sanger. In 1913, before embarking on her educational and legal campaigns, she had combed Europe in the hope of finding acceptable methods of birth control. Except for the diaphragm, she had come back with very little useful information.

The diaphragm is an excellent form of contraception for some, if not all, women. But when thirty-five years passed without the advent of alternate methods, Margaret Sanger decided to look into the matter. She was particularly interested in the development of an oral contraceptive, a pill that women could take easily, and when her friend and colleague Dr. Abraham Stone arranged a meeting with Gregory Pincus, she lost no time in entrusting him with her mission.

After having told him of the botched and self-inflicted abortions that still took a heavy toll among the poor the world over, she went over to the attack, "It is about time you scientists did something about this disgraceful situation."

Pincus, as so many before him, was won over almost instantly by this charming and resolute reformer. He told her that such a contraceptive was conceivable on theoretical grounds, but that it would require money to purchase all the material, engage staff and obtain thousands of mice, rats and rabbits.

"A few weeks after this conversation," he recalled, "I received a note from Mrs. Sanger, which said: 'I have 2,000 dollars, perhaps a little more, will this do?' The amount was ludicrous, but I at once replied 'Yes.' Some days after that I received a check for 2,300 dollars."

Fortunately, the ground work for the Pill had already been laid. Nature has evolved its creatures in such a manner that they will only develop one crop or set of offspring at a time. Most higher mammals will instinctively refuse any male once they have conceived, and some, such as the house mouse, will even abort spontaneously if they so much as smell another "man" around the house.

The overt or instinctive behavior of the pregnant female has, however, nothing moral or intellectual about it. In the lowly mouse as well as in the highly developed woman it is all taken care of by a subtle interplay of hormones. Two different mechanisms operate according to whether the female *has conceived* or should be *readied to conceive.*

In women the body prepares itself once every twenty-eight days for fertilization. The initial signal is given by the pituitary, which emits the follicle-stimulating hormone. As its name implies, it stimulates the ovary to ripen a follicle and to produce estrogen. (See chart page 68.)

MENSTRUAL CYCLE APPROXIMATE

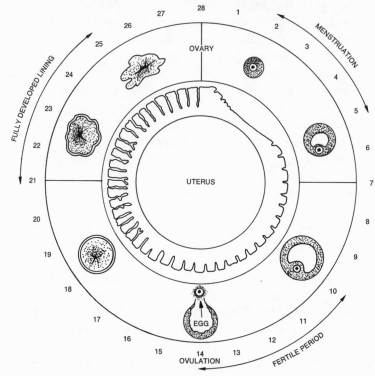

DAYS		Gonadotropins FSH,+ LH	Estrogen	Progesterone	Lining of Uterus (Endometium)	Follicle	Corpus Luteum
1-5	Menstruation	↗			Shedding	Primordial follicle starts maturing egg	
6-13		↗	↗	↗	Building up		
11-14	Fertile period	max.	↗	↗		↓	
14	Ovulation	↘	max.	maximum	↗	Mature egg released	Corpus luteum develops in empty follicle
15-21		↘	↘		maximum	Egg travels through tubes	Young corpus luteum
22-25		↗	↘	↘	↘	Ready for implantation	Mature corpus luteum
25-28		↗		↘	↘	Starts to break down	Degenerated egg	Degenerated corpus luteum

Arrows denote increases and decreases of hormone production.

The amount of estrogen produced by the ovary increases daily. Since estrogen and FSH work in a seesaw fashion, the presence of increasing amounts of estrogen in the blood "tells" the pituitary to curtail FSH production, and estrogen also participates in preparing the uterus for pregnancy.

It takes the ovary ten to sixteen days to ripen an ovum. At ovulation the ovum ruptures the wall of the ovary, enters the fallopian tube, and proceeds downward toward the uterus. The journey takes three to four days, and it is during this time that the egg can be fertilized.

In addition to FSH the pituitary also makes a second sex hormone. It is called the lutenizing hormone (LH) because it specifically triggers the development of the corpus luteum, the yellow body that fills the cavity in the follicle left by the ovum. The corpus luteum is a temporary hormone production plant, designed to make progesterone—the hormone of pregnancy or gestation. Indeed, progesterone immediately signals the uterus to complete the soft lining whose growth had been initiated by estrogen.

If the ovum, on its way to the uterus, becomes fertilized, production of the primary sex hormones, estrogen and progesterone, remains high, and FSH and LH production remains suppressed.

If, however, the ovum is not fertilized, estrogen production by the ovary drops off. The now superfluous corpus luteum disintegrates, and progesterone production is curtailed. Without the support of progesterone, the uterus sheds its lining, which appears as menstrual blood.

The absence of estrogen and progesterone triggers the pituitary into action. FSH and LH production is stepped up, a new follicle starts to mature, and the cycle repeats itself.

One obvious way to prevent conception would be to keep a woman in a state of pseudo-pregnancy by artificially maintaining a high level of progesterone and estrogen.

It was known that administration of progesterone inhibits ovulation in many species, and it was of these experiments that Pincus thought when he told Margaret Sanger that oral contraception was indeed a theoretical possibility.

Pincus knew that he needed the help of many scientists if he was to turn Margaret Sanger's dream into reality. One of the first he

Min-Chueh Chang

recruited was Dr. Min-Chueh Chang, a young Chinese scientist who had come to the Worcester Foundation in 1945.

Reminiscing about the early days of oral contraception, Pincus said:

Chang has an extraordinary gift for experimentation. It seems as though he can feel in advance how the animals will react to a given product. Without him, my researches would not have taken such a definite direction, and it would have been impossible for me to control all the hypotheses that I formulated.

Dr. Chang began by studying the effect of progesterone on ovulation and fertilization in the rabbit. One group of females was injected with small amounts of progesterone; the others received the hormone in tablet form.

Much to Chang's annoyance the rabbits did not understand that they were about to make medical history and spat out the tablets. Dr. Chang, however, had the last word. He dissolved the progesterone and gave it to the stubborn beasts by stomach tube.

After the animals had been medicated for a number of weeks, they were mated. For rabbits, progesterone accomplished its intended purpose. By inhibiting ovulation, it was a 100 percent effective biological contraceptive. Its action was reversible: When the treatment was discontinued, the does resumed breeding in rabbitlike fashion, without any apparent ill effects.

But a contraceptive that worked in the laboratory for a handful of rabbits was not the same thing as one that was to be used by millions of women. Pincus and Chang knew that they had only begun.

At this point the efforts of the scientists at the Worcester Foundation were augmented by those of Dr. John Rock, a gynecologist who worked in nearby Brookline, Massachusetts.

Dr. Rock, who at the time was past sixty years old, has the bearing, look, and indignation one associates with a prophet of the Old Testament. Few listeners fail to shudder when he speaks of "the hand of the Recording Angel, which already is poised to write that: 'through individual stupidity, selfishness, and sloth, Man has reproduced himself back into savagery.'"

Actually John Rock is one of the gentlest of creatures, deeply concerned with the fate of his fellow-men. He only reluctantly witnesses the hunger and misery that beset so much of humanity. Some years ago, when he went to Bombay and saw how the poor were lying in the streets, he became so despondent that he refused to visit Calcutta and other parts of India. "I had seen enough," he said, and went home to the Pilgrim State where he had been born and worked all his life.

The fact that John Rock became a physician, a gynecologist, and a fervent advocate of birth control seems unlikely at first.

As he is fond of telling, he started out as a businessman, and only the fact that he was totally incompetent—he was fired by the United Fruit Company in Guatemala and by an engineering firm in

Boston—decided him to enter Harvard College at the ripe old age of twenty-one.

He went to medical school and decided to specialize in psychiatry. A thorough man, Rock felt that he would not be able to comprehend the working of the female mind unless he became familiar with reproduction. He thus started his psychiatric specialization by becoming an obstetric resident at Boston's Lying-In Hospital. When his residency was completed, he felt so old that he thought it about time to practice and support himself. Boston seemed the ideal spot.

But medical practice and a professorship at Harvard was not enough for John Rock. He also headed a major laboratory research program. Like so many others whose story is told here, he was

John Rock

72

fascinated by the mammalian egg. In 1936, after reading Aldous Huxley's *Brave New World,* in which babies are hatched in bottles, he decided to attempt fertilizing the human ovum *in vitro.* (This refers to the fact that laboratory ware is usually made out of glass, or vitrum. The expression now always means "in the laboratory" as compared to *in vivo,* or "in the living body.")

His collaborator, Mrs. Miriam F. Menkin, also had a long-standing emotional tie to the mammalian egg, since her father had studied biology at the University of Dorpat in Russia, where von Baer so long ago had been the first to see the elusive ovum.

Ova for the fertilization experiments were to come from ovaries that had to be removed surgically for medical reasons. The operations were scheduled to coincide with the ovulation time of the patients, and every Wednesday Miriam Menkin waited outside the operating room for suitable ovaries. Then she spent hours hunting for mature ova. Once found, the ova were mixed with sperm cells and incubated.

For six years Mrs. Menkin worked in vain, but one Friday in 1944, when she examined her preparations, she beheld a novel sight. At first she thought that she was suffering from double vision, but her eyes were not playing tricks, and she indeed saw "the most beautiful sight ever." The single-celled ovum had split in two. But the triumph was not yet complete, for she lost the "two-cell egg" during the fixation procedure. Even now, more than a quarter of a century later, she still feels as if she had had a miscarriage in vitro.

Fortunately she seemed to have developed a knack for in vitro fertilization. A week later another ovum divided. It was fixed successfully and now is part of the Carnegie Foundation's exhibit of very young embryos, which were collected by Dr. Rock and Dr. Arthur T. Hertig over a period of sixteen years.

These scientific achievements notwithstanding, most of John Rock's energy was devoted to his patients. His speciality within a speciality was infertility. In 1924 he had helped reactivate the infertility clinic of Massachusetts General Hospital, and he has been operating such a center ever since. When the time came for him to retire from the staff of the Free Hospital in Boston and he was made Clinical Professor Emeritus of the Harvard Medical School, he organized the Rock Reproductive Center in Brookline, where he and his staff—including Mrs. Menkin—looked after many infertile couples.

73

In his treatment of infertility Rock had noted that the uteri and oviducts of many who were infertile for no apparent reason were underdeveloped. Reasoning that since these structures increase in size during the early months of pregnancy when the body is flooded with sex hormones, Rock had put a small group of patients on a combined estrogen-progesterone regime. He hoped that this would stimulate the growth of the reproductive organs.

Describing these experiments years later, Dr. Rock recalled:

Eighty childless patients agreed to try treatment with added natural hormones, known to be harmless. Daily, for three months, they took massive doses of them. The women had some of the signs and symptoms of a genuine pregnancy. For instance, they did not menstruate during the months of treatment, the breasts and, in some cases, the uterus seemed to become larger. After treatment was discontinued, menstruation recurred, and within four months, thirteen of the women became pregnant. This was quite encouraging, for one could hardly have expected 16 percent of the patients, with long standing infertility of unknown cause, to conceive all within four months of the same treatment.

At first Rock was unaware that Gregory Pincus, in nearby Worcester, was using progesterone for exactly the opposite purpose: trying to keep rabbits from conceiving. It was, however, not long before the two scientists shared their experiences.

They were old friends, their paths having crossed often at Harvard, at various scientific meetings, and in the laboratory. At one time Dr. Pincus, like Mrs. Menkin, had waited patiently while Rock was operating, so as to obtain ovaries for his research.

Both were also concerned with the fate of humanity. Even though Rock is an ardent and practicing Catholic, he feels very strongly that "the time has come" for his church to change its stand on birth control. His conviction ripened during the more than forty years he spent practicing as a gynecologist. He had started to deliver babies even before he was a full-fledged physician. As he recalled in 1963:

As a medical student I was promptly exposed to life in the raw when I acted as midwife to women known to be undergoing normal childbirth. A typical experience was in a three-room tenement where a mother of four was laboring to deliver her fifth. I had only the harassed young father to assist me, with what little time and energy the care of four lively young ones could spare him. I was there from noon until after midnight. Ten fairly similar cases in the third year and more in my last year of school gave me an utterly realistic view of many important aspects of human sexuality.

Dr. Rock knew that the rhythm method, the only birth-control practice sanctioned by the Catholic Church, did not work sufficiently well, and he was prepared to help develop another technique that would be acceptable to members of his faith. Since natural hormones seemed to fulfill all the requirements, he agreed to become the medical man on Gregory Pincus' team.

Pincus and Chang had shown that progesterone was an effective contraceptive for rabbits. Since this was not the final aim of the study, they were eager to try their biological method on women. In its experimental state it could, however, hardly be recommended to those who wanted to practice birth control. Rock's infertile patients, on the other hand, were an ideal stepping stone for testing whether progesterone suppressed ovulation. (Ovulation, and its absence, can be detected by various laboratory tests.)

Instead of using a combination of estrogens and progesterone, as he had done previously, Rock, at Pincus' suggestion, used only progesterone. Furthermore, in order to cause menstruation even though no egg would be released (this is called withdrawal bleeding), the patients were instructed to take progesterone for only twenty days of the month (from day 5 to day 25). Pincus expected the women to menstruate four to five days after medication was discontinued.

Rock selected a new group of twenty-seven women with long-standing infertility. He prescribed 300 mg of progesterone a day for twenty days, the course to be repeated for a total of up to four months. Menstruation set in "on time," as Pincus had predicted. Progesterone alone was as effective as progesterone plus estrogen. The Rock rebound, as the effect had been called, still worked. Four out of the twenty-seven women conceived within six months after progesterone had been discontinued. This was again significantly higher than expected by chance alone.

Rock and Pincus were, however, not quite satisfied. When taken orally, the effective doses of progesterone were extremely high. Moreover, Rock was bothered by the fact the progesterone caused "breakthrough" bleeding (slight bleeding between menstrual periods) in 20 per cent of the patients. For Pincus progesterone treatment was not "safe" enough. Ovulation was suppressed in 85 per cent of the cases only.

Since scientists first began using hormones for medicinal purposes, it had become apparent that synthetic hormones differing slightly in their chemical structure from their natural counterparts are sometimes more effective than the natural hormone itself. This might be due to the fact that the natural hormone often controls several physiological processes, whereas the man-made counterpart can be tailored to control only one. Whatever the reason, it seemed worthwhile to search for a better pill.

In this endeavor Rock, Pincus, and Chang could expect help from other quarters. Since hormones and hormonelike substances had wrought unexpected medical miracles, the research departments of the big pharmaceutical houses were continuously synthesizing and testing compounds that would, they hoped, fill a medical need or improve on nature.

Searle and Co. was particularly interested in developing a synthetic with progesteronelike activity that could be taken orally. Compounds having a particular chemical configuration (19-norsteroid) seemed particularly promising, and two of these, bearing laboratory numbers SC-5914 and SC-4642, were among the more than two hundred samples that the pharmaceutical companies shipped to the Worcester Foundation when Pincus called for steroids.

Dr. Chang and his staff tested each one of these on an army of rats, mice, and rabbits. First, groups of females were dosed with the test compound at various concentrations, then they were mated, and finally the number of young was counted.

All during the autumn of 1953 Chang kept at his laboratory bench. Gradually the two hundred-odd compounds were narrowed down to fifteen. Then only three remained, among them the two 19-norsteroids received from Searle and a third, norethindrone, which also belonged to this chemical group. After only a few tests there was no doubt that this trio was dramatically superior to any other substance tested.

Victory was in sight, for the 19-norsteroids seemed to fill all the requirements of a biological contraceptive. They inhibited ovulation in all cases. When taken orally, they were ten times as powerful as progesterone, and the women had thus to take only a small amount of medication. Their effect was temporary. Rats and rabbits that had been on 19-norsteroid therapy for months gave birth to completely normal litters once medication was discontinued. Today, all synthetic substances with progesterone-like activity are collectively referred to as progestins.

For the moment Dr. Chang and his rabbits had done all they could. The next move again was up to Rock, his right-hand man, Dr. Celso Ramon de Garcia, and their infertile patients. For the third time a group of suitable infertile women were asked whether they would try an experimental drug.

Fifty patients volunteered. For women, as for animals, the 19-norsteroids proved much more active than progesterone. Instead of daily doses of 300 mg of the natural hormone, they needed only 10 to 15 mg of 19-norsteroids. The new compounds also caused considerably less nausea and other side effects than progesterone. Moreover, they can be taken orally. When taken as instructed from day 5 to day 25, a normal menstrual flow was maintained. When discontinued, ovulation was resumed, and six out of these fifty highly infertile patients became pregnant within two to six months.

It took great courage to test the Pill for its contraceptive activity on large groups of normal, fertile women. What if it did not work? What if it worked too well and if prolonged use rendered women permanently sterile? What if it proved harmful to the unborn? What if it undermined the health of the mother? What if . . . ?

The history of medicine bears witness to risks taken in the past. Anesthesia, widespread vaccination against smallpox, polio, diphtheria, and measles, chlorination of drinking water, iodization of salt—all were at one time a great step into the unknown fully justified by the need they would fill if successful. So it was with the birth-control pill.

In their search for a suitable testing ground the fathers of the Pill had come upon Puerto Rico. The lovely island in the Caribbean Sea was a miniature example of the population explosion. Modern medicine had arrived, in 1898, when the island was taken over by the United States. The death rate dropped and the population rose dramatically.

Little, however, was done to develop Puerto Rico's meager agricultural and industrial resources, and by the 1950's the island was plunged into poverty. Illiteracy and semiliteracy were high. Families were large, and the majority of the women had all the children they wanted when they were still at the height of their reproductive powers.

The population had also grown accustomed to receiving medical care from public-health clinics. Follow-ups would not be too difficult. In spite of the fact that the island was predominantly Catholic, its plight was so severe that birth control was legalized in 1937. Even before the Pill was ready to be tested, Dr. Abraham Stone and other officials of the Planned Parenthood Federation had gone to Puerto Rico to help it resolve its population crisis.

The first field trials were carried out in Puerto Rico by Dr. Edris Rice Wray, medical director of the local Family Planning Association. She chose a housing development in Río Piedras, which had a relatively stable population.

Groundwork for the tests was laid carefully. Each prospective participant was visited by a social worker who explained the purpose of the investigation, and if the patient consented, gave her a month's supply of oral contraceptives. The pills were to be taken from day 5 to day 25. Thereafter, the patient was to receive another set.

The Pill (Searle's Norethynodrel) was almost 100 per cent effective. Of the 221 women who completed the six-month test, and who ordinarily produced a child a year, only a handful became pregnant. A careful analysis of the failure always turned up a human error, such as a skipped pill or a misunderstanding. When questioned, one woman admitted that she had taken the pills only when her husband was at home. Another conceived even though her husband had faithfully taken a pill a day!

At this point in the history of oral contraception, a small oversight that had occurred in the manufacture of the early batches of Norethynodrel was put to good use.

Rock had noted that there was a certain amount of breakthrough bleeding when he switched his infertile patients from the combined estrogen-progesterone therapy to pure progesterone. This problem had not occurred with Searle's early pills, but appeared, quite often, when the investigators started to use later shipments.

Close investigation of this mystery indicated that the early batches had been contaminated by a trace of estrogen. One part of estrogen was henceforth added to sixty-six parts of Norethynodrel, and the first Pill—Enovid—was ready.

The Pill has been with us for more than fifteen years. The first small field trial in San Juan was rapidly followed by large-scale ones in Puerto Rico, Haiti, and Los Angeles, and today oral contraceptives are widely used.

Their side and long-term effects continue to be investigated by scientists all over the world, and the final answers will not be in until the women who have been on the Pill for extended periods of time will have come to the end of their natural life. (It is good to remember here that it took forty years until the correlation between cigarette smoking and lung cancer was established.)

So far, fortunately, few long-term side effects have emerged, except for a slight increase in certain thromboembolic (blood-clotting) diseases, and oral contraceptives are not prescribed for women who have a history of such conditions.

Yet certain animal experiments, as well as long-term side effects of related estrogens, have made physicians increasingly reluctant to keep women on hormones for long periods of time.

Oral contraceptives—like most medications—are double-edged swords, and this is why there is a constant search for alternate methods of birth control and for pills that contain even smaller doses of hormones.

8
A Taboo Method Comes into Its Own

Few people are indifferent to death, even when, as in the case of doctors, they meet it frequently as part of their profession. When death comes to the old or the very ill, it is acceptable, but not when it is needless.

It was such deaths that shaped the career of Alan F. Guttmacher while he was still only an intern at Johns Hopkins University Hospital in Baltimore during the 1920's.

Medically speaking this was eons ago, during the preantibiotic age, when all infections, including those resulting from botched or self-inflicted abortions, were often fatal. So it was that Alan Guttmacher could not help effectively when a young black girl of fifteen was admitted with a galloping uterine infection and a fever of 105° caused by an illegal abortion. A hysterectomy, which seemed the only possible way of saving this child, was performed, but she nevertheless died four hours after the operation.

The young were not the only ones affected by ignorance and uncertain methods of birth control. Dr. Guttmacher saw one woman in her mid-forties who mistook the onset of menopause for

Alan F. Guttmacher

another unwanted pregnancy. She went to a local abortionist, and also died of complications.

"Death is usually kind," Dr. Guttmacher said recently. "It is preceded by a dulling of the senses, or by coma. But I recall one woman, by the name of Knight, bleeding to death from an abortion. She remained conscious until five minutes before the end, pleading for life in words that still ring in my ears."

Thus aroused, he started to investigate the birth pattern of those that had their offspring at Johns Hopkins.

The hospital then was not integrated. Private patients were housed at the top on Floor B-4. Twelve feet below were the white wards, and below that were the black ones. The number of babies born to the occupants of these floors varied inversely with their economic and social status.

The private patients came back once, twice, or three times at regularly spaced intervals. The white ward patients returned more often, five to six times in all, whereas the black patients came once a year, regular as clockwork.

Dr. Guttmacher was puzzled by these figures, and asked his more experienced colleagues for an explanation.

"Yes," he was told, "there are great racial and class differences in fertility. Men who work with their brains have weak spermatozoa. Those that use their brawn have much more powerful seed."

Guttmacher was not quite convinced and started to research the subject in the library. There he came across a revolutionary book by a Dr. Bebee, who stated that the differences in fertility observed between races and classes was a matter of birth control.

Guttmacher sided with Dr. Bebee, and devoted much of his professional energy to seeing that everyone could have "babies by choice," and not by chance.

He specialized in obstetrics and remained at Johns Hopkins in Baltimore. Then he moved to Mount Sinai Hospital in New York City. Finally, in 1962, he became the president of the Planned Parenthood-World Population Association.

By then birth control had ceased to be a private matter between the anxious patient and the concerned physician or social worker. Survival of the world was linked to stemming the worldwide population explosion.

One of Dr. Guttmacher's first tasks as president was to evaluate, in person, the progress made both nationally and internationally.

To his dismay, he discovered that oral contraceptives, which worked so well when they were administered under close medical supervision, were unsuccessful in India and Southeast Asia. As he reported:

I came back with the firm conviction that the reason the restraint of population growth in these areas is moving so slowly is the fact that the methods we offer are Western methods, methods poorly suited to their culture and to the control of mass-population growth.

Our methods are largely birth control for the individual, not birth control for a nation. Therefore, I felt very strongly that new methods must be offered and, if the new methods are good and proper, results will be astounding.

One of the "new" methods Guttmacher had in mind was the IUD—short for intrauterine (contraceptive) device. IUD's were really not new at all, their use had just been taboo.

Dr. Guttmacher, and other birth controllers, like to relate that Arab camel drivers placed small round pebbles into the wombs of their camels so as to keep them barren on their long treks through the desert.

Though this story is true, the human version of the IUD is the direct descendant of the stem pessaries that were popular during the early part of this century as contraceptive devices, and the doctor who developed the ancestor of today's IUD probably never knew that camels practiced birth control so successfully.

One of the most popular stem pessaries was developed by Dr. Karl Pust in 1923. It consisted of a button that protruded into the vagina and a stem that filled the cervical canal. So that the device would stay put, Pust attached a few loops of catgut, a widely used surgical suturing material, to the stem end of the pessary. These threads hung into the uterine cavity. The device worked, so Pust thought, because it mechanically sealed off the cervix and thus prevented the sperm cells from reaching the uterus.

The Pust pessary was designed to remain in place. It had, however, to be removed at regular intervals by a gynecologist and this occupied a fair share of the time of some doctors, among them Ernst Gräefenberg, who had a fashionable practice in Berlin.

Contraception is only a small part of a gynecologist's work, and so it was that Dr. Gräefenberg was consulted by a young woman who had trouble conceiving. As a first step Gräefenberg did a D and C—short for dilation and curettage. The operation consists of dilating the cervical canal by means of a series of probes and scraping the uterus with a "curette," a blunt instrument that looks somewhat like an ice-cream spoon.

When Gräefenberg examined the material he had removed from the uterus of his patient, he noticed a few strands of catgut that must originally have been attached to a Pust pessary the woman had been wearing before she opted for motherhood.

The D and C apparently did the trick, because the patient returned pregnant a few months after the procedure.

Louis Pasteur was fond of saying that "chance favors the prepared mind." It did so in this instance, for instead of dismissing this routine case from his mind, Gräefenberg saw in it the germ of a

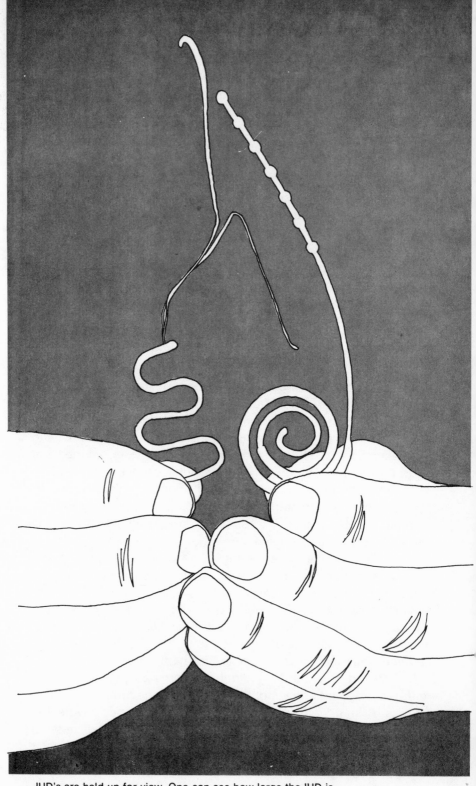

IUD's are held up for view. One can see how large the IUD is.

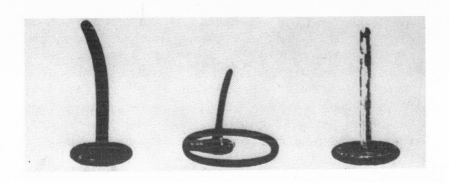

Pust and stem pessaries.

85

new contraceptive method, one that consisted of introducing a few strands of string, which could be removed at any time, into the uterine cavity of the woman.

At the time antibiotics had not been discovered, and uterine infections were a dreaded complication of gynecological and obstetric practice. Gräefenberg reasoned that a contraceptive device, like the one he was planning to develop, which would lie entirely within the uterine cavity, might be much safer than one, like the Pust pessary, connecting the "clean and sterile" uterus with the "microbe infested" vagina.

Before this could be decided, the method had to be tested. Gräefenberg fashioned some IUD's out of silkworm gut, which was another popular surgical suturing material, and in the mid-1920's recruited some volunteers from his thriving practice.

The first IUD model he tried consisted of three short strands of silkworm gut, knotted into a star. These silk stars were easily expelled, but rings made out of coiled material fared much better, especially after Gräefenberg reinforced them with a fine silver wire. Gradually the silkworm gut was discarded, and Gräefenberg began using coils made of pure silver or gold wire. At first the rings, which were manufactured by a local watchmaker, came in several sizes; then Gräefenberg decided that one size (17.5 mm diameter) fitted most women.

There was no doubt that the rings were effective contraceptives, but were they safe? Gräefenberg had avoided infection by working under strictly sterile conditions during insertion and removal, and by rejecting anyone with any sign of infection or venereal disease.

There remained the possibility that IUD's caused local changes in the uterus that might eventually become malignant. To rule this out, Gräefenberg asked one of Germany's leading pathologists to examine small samples of uterine tissue under the microscope (such a procedure is called a biopsy). No adverse changes were noted in biopsy material taken from women who had worn IUD's for extended periods of time.

Gräefenberg, proud and pleased with his discovery, presented a report on his IUD at the Congress of the German Gynecological Society, which met in Frankfurt in 1931.

The paper was greeted with furor. Gräefenberg's colleagues wondered how a self-respecting gynecologist could dare to place a "foreign body" deep inside the delicate womb of a woman. Even if by some miracle it did not cause an inflammation, it would almost certainly rupture the uterine wall, they said.

One of the most apalled was Dr. Selmar Aschheim, who together with Bernhard Zondek had just published the pregnancy test that would prove so important to the sex-hormone hunters.

Gräefenberg, however, remained undaunted, and continued to use the ring for both the elegant patients who came to call at his fashionable office on Berlin's famous Kurfürstendamm and those less well endowed who consulted him at his clinic in Neukölln, a working-class suburb of Berlin. Since he also firmly believed that no woman should unwillingly bear a child, he performed abortions on demand.

Gräefenberg publicized the IUD and attracted the attention of Margaret Sanger, who was constantly looking for newer and better methods of contraception. She invited him to address the Seventh International Birth Control Congress held in Zurich, Switzerland.

The Nazis came to power in Germany in 1933. Since they wanted large families for their projected thousand-year Reich, they put an end to the German birth-control movement. The time had also come for the Jews to leave "the Fatherland." But Gräefenberg refused to see the writing on the wall. He felt secure and protected, because his practice included the wives of many highly placed party officials.

Like so many others, he misjudged the situation and was arrested in 1938. Apparently he had been denounced by a jilted mistress who claimed that he had smuggled a valuable postage stamp out of Germany.

The Nazis, forever short of foreign currency, were ready to let him go provided that his American friends would put up ransom money in dollars. Negotiations were initiated, and within a matter of months Margaret Sanger had raised enough cash to buy Gräefenberg's freedom. He arrived in New York City in 1939.

At first he questioned whether he could make a living in New York, and he contemplated moving to Chicago, a city less choked with refugee doctors. But a colleague, Dr. Hans Lehfeldt, who as a young physician had witnessed the storm at the German Gynecological Congress, persuaded him to stay. It was sound advice, and Gräefenberg's practice on Park Avenue flourished.

In the beginning Margaret Sanger also helped. She relaxed her strict rules against "no men," and let Gräefenberg work, in a minor capacity, at the Margaret Sanger Research Bureau.

Though Gräefenberg continued to believe that IUD's were the best available methods of contraception, he never prescribed them while he practiced in the United States, since their use was considered malpractice.

There is, however, some indirect evidence that IUD's continued to be used by some doctors, since once in a while an indignant physician reported that he had recovered a "foreign body" from the uterus of a patient.

One of these doctors who developed a stainless-steel version of the coiled ring was Gräefenberg's pupil, Herbert H. Hall, a refugee from Czechoslovakia.

Dr. Hall and the others who must have perpetrated such sins were very silent about their endeavors, but one woman gynecologist, Dr. Mary Halton, who practiced on Madison Avenue in Manhattan, was bold enough to talk about it openly. In 1948 Robert L. Dickinson, founder of the National Committee on Maternal Health and a renowned and respected member of the medical profession, persuaded her to publish her results.

The paper, entitled "Contraception With an Intrauterine Silk Coil," appeared in the October 1948 issue of *Human Fertility.* It was signed by Dr. Halton, Dr. Dickinson, and Dr. Christopher Tietze—another newcomer to these shores who recalled much later, "I frankly admit that I would not have dared to attach my name to so subversive a piece of medical literature, had I not had the encouragement of the venerable Robert L. Dickinson."

The paper did not cause much of a stir, and another decade was to pass before intrauterine devices were again in the limelight. This time they were to be investigated at the request of the editors of the *American Journal of Obstetrics and Gynecology.*

However, when the editors searched for a physician who would do the evaluation, they could not find any American gynecologist willing to deal with this controversial subject. Finally, the study was carried out by W. Oppenheimer, a gynecologist who, after having used a Gräefenberg-type ring in Germany, had taken IUD's with him to Israel.

His paper, published in 1959, evaluated the use of IUD's in 329 different subjects who used the device for a combined period of

793 years. The failure rate was calculated to be 2.5 pregnancies per 100 years exposure. Oppenheimer, who had used the method continuously from 1930 on, considered it to be entirely harmless.

The same year that Oppenheimer's report was published in America, a similar paper appeared in Japan. The author, Dr. Atsumi Ishihama, had used an Ota ring (a variant of the Gräefenberg ring) for some time. Since the report was favorable and thus conflicted with the official stand of Japanese medicine, it must have taken courage on the part of Ishihama, a young university professor, to publish it. To make matters worse, Dr. Ota had been ostracized because of his leftist political associations, and his ring had become associated with unpopular causes.

Unpopular or not, time was ripe for a re-evaluation of the matter, and it was to this end that Alan Guttmacher called for an International Conference on Intrauterine Devices to be held in New York City a bare two months after his return from the Far East.

Scientists are busy people, and international meetings are usually planned years in advance. This one, however, was put together in a hurry by the Population Council, which had been established in 1952 almost single-handedly by John D. Rockefeller III, "to stimulate, encourage, promote, conduct, and support significant activities in the broad field of population." Christopher Tietze, who had signed his name to the only IUD paper that appeared in America during the twenty years of the device's underground existence, by now was on the staff of the Population Council, as were Frank W. Notestein, Sheldon J. Segal, and other scientists who played an important role in American contraceptive research.

The First International Conference on IUD's was convened on April 30, 1962. Attendance was small. Only forty-eight persons were called to order by chairman Guttmacher, but the list reads like a Who's Who in IUD's. The most notable absence was that of Ernst Gräefenberg, who, in the words of one participant, "never lived to see the acknowledgment of the value of his great idea." But others who had continued to believe in the usefulness of IUD's were there. W. Oppenheimer had come from Israel and Atsumi Ishihama from Japan. There were Hans Lehfeldt, the long-time associate and personal friend of Gräefenberg's, Herbert H. Hall, his American student, and Margaret Jackson, who had used IUD's for problem patients in England even though she had been taught as a student "that fitting such things was devil's work."

Then there were those who had started working with IUD's in the late 1950's. One of these was Lazar C. Margulies, working at Mount Sinai Hospital in New York. As he recalled:

My interest in contraceptives was aroused by Dr. John Rock of Boston who, in November 1958 delivered the I. C. Rubin Memorial Lecture at Mount Sinai Hospital.

I was taken aback by the incongruity of this distinguished scientist's topic for the occasion. I expected to hear about new discoveries and progress in the treatment of sterility, which was Isidor Rubin's main aim in life. To my surprise, Dr. Rock spoke for more than an hour about the dire consequences of overpopulation and the urgent necessity for large-scale conception control.

The lecture gave me the incentive to search for a simple, inexpensive, and reliable permanent contraceptive that could be applied and removed easily. I knew of the Gräefenberg ring and that doctors did apply it here, but I did not feel that it lived up to all demands. . . .

Dr. Margulies' chief at Mount Sinai was Alan Guttmacher, who was more than happy to let him experiment with better contraceptive devices.

Since Gräefenberg's days inert plastics, which interact even less with the body than gold, had become available. Dr. Margulies made a few IUD's from thin polyethylene tubing and proceeded to test them on a few selected volunteers.

The results were disappointing. The devices caused bleeding, were painful to insert, and were expelled by 40 per cent of the patients. Progress obviously could not be achieved in such a hurry, and Margulies returned to his drawing board. The doctor now turned designer. For a year he experimented with different types of plastic and a variety of shapes and forms.

Early in his research he had abandoned the traditional ring. Insertion of IUD's through the narrow cervical canal had always been difficult and painful, since the devices had to be big enough to fill the uterine cavity. Insertion would be much easier if the device could be introduced as a flat strip. Since plastics "remember" the shape they are given during molding, the devices resume their coiled shape inside the uterus. To keep the strips flat during insertion, Margulies placed them inside a thin plastic tube, equipped with a plunger. At the appropriate time the plunger is pushed down, and the tube ejects the IUD much as a syringe delivers its content of medicine.

Modern IUD's. They come in various shapes. The latest ones contain copper.

After experimenting with a variety of shapes—a beaded S; a plain double S; a beaded double S; loops; and pretzels—Margulies finally settled on a spiral.

One more problem remained to be solved. One of the chief drawbacks of IUD's is that they are spontaneously ejected by up to 20 per cent of the patients. Since the great advantage of the method is that it requires no care once in place, such expulsions are often undetected.

Because IUD's are labeled with radiopaque dyes, their presence and correct emplacement can be ascertained by x-ray, but this is an office procedure. Margulies wanted to find a way for his patients to check their IUD's at home.

A string of seven plastic beads, attached to the open end of the IUD, was the answer. By counting the three beads that were supposed to protrude into the vagina, a woman could tell whether her IUD was in its proper place.

Whereas Massachusetts had been the home of the Pill, New York State became the testing ground for the IUD. While Margulies experimented with spirals, Jack Lippes, an assistant professor of gynecology at the State University of New York at Buffalo, also experimented with intrauterine contraception.

His interest was prompted by a private patient who, in spite of using a diaphragm, had had ten children in ten years. As he said: "I decided we needed something better."

At first Lippes experimented with the classic Gräefenberg and Ota rings, but found them far from ideal. Both insertion and removal were too difficult. Some initial modifications facilitated insertion, but removal remained a problem. Lippes became so experienced at extracting rings with Graefenberg's blunt crochet-type hook that his nurses at the Planned Parenthood Center in Buffalo dubbed him the "Jimmy Valentine of the Contraceptive World."

A contraceptive device for mass consumption, however, could not rest on such talents, and Lippes also started to develop his own IUD. Like Margulies, he tried various plastics and different shapes and ended up with the "Lippes' loop," which he showed to his colleagues at the First International Congress on Intrauterine IUD's.

This meeting ended on a note of hope. Much more was known about IUD's than one could have expected, given the lack of recognition they had received in the past. But much more had to be known before IUD's could be applied on a worldwide basis.

IUD's worked, but how? Those who had used the method had dealt with small, selected groups of patients. Could the devices be inserted—assembly-line fashion—by a team of doctors or nurses? IUD's had been produced by hand or at best on a small scale; factories would be needed for mass production. Which one of the current models was the best, or had the best not yet been developed? Thirty years earlier the medical world had rejected IUD's as unsafe because they might cause infections or pierce the uterine wall. Limited usage, presented by a few physicians, indicated otherwise. More research and large-scale statistical analysis would be needed to substantiate their findings as well as to evaluate the efficiency of the method.

And then there were the actual clinical problems. What was the best time of the month for insertion? How often should a woman be re-examined? What was one to do about those who expelled the IUD's, those who experienced pain, those who had too heavy a menstrual flow? Should they be dropped from the program, or could they perhaps be fitted with a larger or smaller size or a different model?

Problems are often solved quickly when the right questions are asked. Christopher Tietze, the Population Council's expert on biomedical statistics, had come prepared with instructions on how to collect meaningful data. (This was the first time in medical history that a method was evaluated from its inception by a completely neutral agency.) Alan Guttmacher cautiously promised financial backing to those seriously interested in carrying out well-controlled studies. Another meeting on IUD's was to be scheduled in a year or two.

It took two and a half years for the group to meet again. By then their ranks had grown from forty-eight to four hundred. Instead of eleven countries the participants now represented thirty-eight. In 1962 the total number of IUD's used throughout the world was a few hundred. In 1964, it was 100,000. In 1962 there were a few isolated clinical programs. By 1964 forty countries had testing programs of various sizes, and three: Korea, Taiwan, and Pakistan, had national ones. Rarely had so much been done so fast.

Many of the questions that were asked when IUD's were in their infancy have been answered today. Large-scale investigations to see whether prolonged usage could cause cancer have proved negative. The number of pelvic infections occurring among patients was insignificant. Close investigation, incidentally, proved that a connection between the uterus and the vagina, as in the case of the Margulies spiral, did not lead to infections. Women who conceived in spite of wearing an IUD gave birth to completely normal infants.

Because it does not involve any hormones or other medication, the IUD has the immense advantage of not interfering with the physiological balance of the body. The effect of the IUD is strictly local, and ovulation remains unaffected. The device, however, has a tendency to cause a heavy menstrual flow, especially during the early months of usage.

The effectiveness of the method is high. Dr. Tietze and his staff analyzed 27,600 cases and determined a failure rate of 1.5 to 3.0 per 100 women during the first year of use. The rate of failure was influenced by the age of the woman, the number of children she had given birth to (some specialists feel that IUD's are not suitable for women who have never borne children), and the type and size of IUD used. Failures were caused by both unnoticed expulsions and conception with the device in place.

Today doctors can chose among many different types of IUD's. In addition to Lippes' loop, Margulies' spiral, Ota's ring, and Zipper's nylon coil, there are Birnberg's bows, Robinson's twin-spiral "safe-T coil," Majzlin's springs, the Butterfly, the Shamrock, and many more. There doubtlessly will be others, for as Frank Notestein, former president of the Population Council, has said concerning the types of intrauterine devices presently available: "We are still at the Model T stage. But Henry Ford built millions of T's before he switched to the Model A."

Intrauterine devices have several advantages over other methods of contraception that make them especially suitable for large-scale application. They are inexpensive, highly effective, and require only a single decision on the part of the patient. Since IUD's require no attention, human errors, such as forgetting to take a pill, are eliminated. Only two women out of one hundred using it for a whole year will become pregnant. Unlike oral contraceptives, IUD's do not interfere with lactation and can thus be used immediately after a mother delivers her baby. This again is important in underdeveloped areas where breast-feeding is often essential for the health of the newborn.

And yet . . . IUD's still do not seem to provide the final solution to the problems of birth control. Older models are expelled by many women during the initial months of use. Other women have to abandon intrauterine devices because they cause pain or bleeding. Others still suffer from pelvic infections. Though IUD's, together with legalized abortions, have brought Japan's birth rate under control and have made inroads into the runaway birth rates of Korea and Taiwan, they have so far failed in India. Thus scientists keep searching for more ways to bridle man's immense natural fertility.

9
Male Methods

Margaret Sanger and her friends founded the American birth-control movement at a time when women throughout the Western world were struggling for political, social, economic, and professional recognition. To a large extent the success of their campaign rested on effective means of family planning, for, as Mrs. Sanger said, "No woman can consider herself free until she can determine the number of children she will bear."

Female methods of birth control were thus emphasized by the fledgling Planned Parenthood Association and for a while research into male methods was neglected.

Traditionally, however, contraception has been a male affair. Apart from cultural reasons, this was so because until twenty years ago all effective methods involved the mechanical separation of sperm and egg.

In the past, the most consistently used means of achieving this end was coitus interruptus, or withdrawal before ejaculation. This form of contraception probably dates back to prehistory and is described in the Bible.

Since procreation was the most important, if not the only, acceptable function of sex, withdrawal was considered sinful by most religious authorities. A rare exception was Rabbi Eliezer who, in the first century A.D., recommended that in the twenty-four months during which a mother nurses her child "the husband thresh within and winnow without" (a poetic way of recommending withdrawal). Religious disapproval notwithstanding, withdrawal was widely used, and today it is still an important method of birth control in many underdeveloped countries.

Coitus interruptus was not the only ancient method of birth control. Sheaths that cover the penis during intercourse are almost as old. Legend has it that the semen of Minos, the powerful king of Crete, contained scorpions and snakes which not only proved injurious to the king's partners but also prevented him from siring a normal heir. Reluctantly he forbore consummation of his marriage to Parsiphae, the beautiful daughter of the King of the Sun.

He finally managed to solve the problem by means of a "fantastic" subterfuge, namely by casting his scorpion-bearing seed into a fresh goat bladder. Thus purged, he could have intercourse with his wife without ill effects, and history records that Parsiphae then bore her husband four sons and four daughters.

This tale demonstrates that animal bladders were used frequently in the ancient world. Usually their purpose was the prevention of disease rather than contraception. In Egypt the sheaths were chiefly worn by bathers so as to ward off the snails that transmit schistosomiasis, a tropical disease that is still rampant in the area today. Egyptian sheaths were dyed in various colors to indicate the social rank of the wearer.

Records of various types of sheaths, including plant pods used by the Chinese, Japanese, and New Guineans, have come down to us, but the first Western account dates from the time of Gabriel Fallopius, the Italian anatomist who described the fallopian tubes in 1564. He also was a great authority on syphilis, then called *morbus Gallicus,* or French disease.

More than four-hundred years ago he initiated what was probably the first controlled study in medicine. At the time Italy and other parts of Europe were forever plunged in armed strife. Armies and camp followers crisscrossed the land, and venereal disease was rampant.

Fallopius discovered that the use of a linen sheath during in-

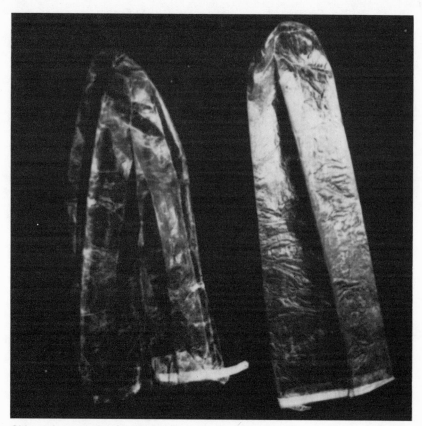

Old condoms made of animal gut.

tercourse prevented infection. The Italian doctor tested the sheath on eleven hundred men and "called immortal God to witness" that not one of them was infected.

Two centuries later a variant of the sheath was used by Casanova, one of the greatest lovers and libertines of all times. By then it had acquired its present name: condom. Medical historians have spent a great deal of time trying to determine the origin of the word. Most believe that the name is derived from the perhaps fictitious family name of a Doctor or Colonel Condom. This English physician attended King Charles II, whose finances were in a disastrous state because of the large number of illegitimate children he was said to have fathered. Other researchers suggest that the name is derived from the small town of Condom in Gascony, a region of France reputed for its high living.

Whatever the truth of the matter, neither the English nor the French wish to be associated with the popularization of the device. Even today it is commonly referred to as a *capote anglaise* (English riding coat) in France and as a "French letter" in England.

During the eighteenth century condoms were made of animal gut. The novel use for this freely available raw material was probably discovered by an inventive butcher.

A great deal of information is available on the lively trade in condoms carried out by a Mrs. Philips. Her shop was located on a small court in ancient London.

Mrs. Philips advertised her products on handbills, one of which is reproduced on the next page.

The lady is emphatic about the quality of her merchandise, and in her handbill she derogates a competitor who used her name to sell an inferior product.

From contemporary accounts one can visualize Mrs. Philip's international clientele. Buyers arrived from Spain, Portugal, France, the Netherlands and other European countries. She sold wholesale to "apothecaries, chymists, and druggists," and also operated a mail order business.

In 1839 the word condom and ten synonyms—Armor, Postocalyptrons, French letter, Cutherean Shield, French Baudruche, Redingote Anglaise, Gant des dames, Calotte d'assurance, Peau divine and Chemisette—appeared in a *New Dictionary of Medical Science and Literature.* The dictionary also describes how to prepare condoms from sheep gut. First the cecum—or blind gut—of a sheep is soaked in water. Then it is turned inside out, scraped, macerated, blown out and dried. Finally it is cut in appropriate lengths that are tied off with fancy ribbons. Contemporary cartoons show gentlemen who amuse themselves by blowing up condoms in the presence of respectable-looking company.

History does not tell how long Mrs. Philips continued to ply her trade in Orange Court. Contemporary accounts state that she had an international clientele including men from France, Spain, and Portugal.

Today condoms are usually made of vulcanized rubber. They are manufactured all over the world in huge quantities—billions of them a year. When used properly, especially in conjunction with a spermicide cream, they are highly effective. They also reduce the incidence of venereal disease.

This advertisement is to inform our customers and others, that the woman who pretended the name of Philips, in Orange-court, is now dead, and that the business is carried on at

Mrs. P H I L I P S's W A R E H O U S E,

That has been for forty years, at the Green Canister, in Bedford (late Half-Moon) Street, seven doors from the Strand, on the left hand side,

STILL continues in its original state of reputation ; where all gentlemen of intrigue may be supplied with those Bladder Policies, or implements of safety, which infallibly secure the health of our customers, superior in quality as has been demonstrated in comparing samples of others that pretend the name of *Philips* ; we defy any one to equal our goods in England, and have lately had several large orders from France, Spain, Portugal, Italy, and other foreign places.

N. B. Ambassadors, foreigners, gentlemen and captains of ships, &c. going abroad, may be supplied with any quantity of the best goods in England, on the shortest notice and lowest price. A most infamous and obscene hand-bill, or advertisement, in the name of *Philips*, is false : the public are hereby assured that their name is not *Philips*, but this is the shop, and the same person is behind the counter as has been for many years.——The following lines are very applicable to our goods :

> *To guard yourself from shame or fear,*
> *Votaries to Venus, hasten here,*
> *None in our wares e'er found a flaw,*
> *Self-preservation's nature's law.*

*** Letters (post paid) duly answered.

Mrs. Philips' handbill.

As in Fallopio's day, the popularity of the "rubber" is due in great part to a war. The U. S. Army distributed condoms free of charge during World War II, and though they were advocated because they protected the troops from VD, their high efficiency as a contraceptive was no secret.

Condoms are an important method of birth control not only in the United States but also in many underdeveloped countries, especially where men are reluctant to abdicate fertility control to their womenfolk.

Even though the manner in which the condom is to be used seems almost self-evident, the following story is told by an Indian family-planning worker.

He had shown the use of condoms by stretching them on a wooden staff for demonstration purposes; then he gave his audience some free samples.

A few months later one of his listeners came back complaining that his wife was pregnant.

"Did you use the condom as you were told?" the instructor asked.

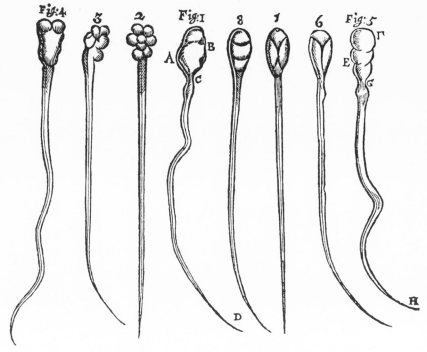

Sperm cells as drawn by Anton van Leeuwenhoek.

"Yes," the man said, "each time we went to bed I stretched the rubber on a wooden staff."

Whether made of skin or rubber, condoms are not to everyone's liking. Madame de Sévigné, a French writer who lived in the seventeenth century, allegedly said that condoms were "armor against pleasure, and cobwebs against danger."

Be this as it may, there has always been a desire to find a substitute male method of contraception. Curiously, until about five years ago, this line of research had been unpopular, partly because of the fact that spermatogenesis (sperm production) is

The sperm factory

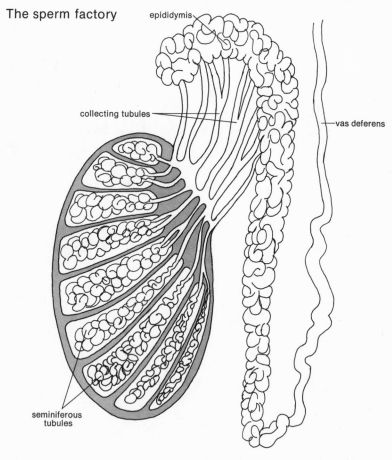

epididymis

collecting tubules

vas deferens

seminiferous tubules

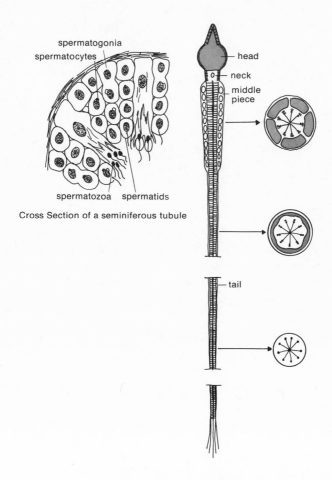

spermatogonia
spermatocytes

spermatozoa   spermatids

Cross Section of a seminiferous tubule

head
neck
middle piece
tail

Though the spermatozoon is the smallest cell of the human body, it is very complex. Its head contains all the necessary genetic information, its tail propels it along its path. An enzyme system attends to housekeeping chores and in the end will assist the sperm to burrow through the outer layers of the ovum.

A highly enlarged view of a mature spermatozoon, as one would see it under an electron microscope. The wall of a seminiferous tubule is shown nearby on a different scale.

very complex. Today, suddenly, the subject has become popular, and scores of scientists are searching for a male pill.

Spermatogenesis takes place in the approximately eight-hundred coiled seminiferous (seed producing) tubules that fill the interior of the testes. Each one of these tubules is about two feet long and as thick as a silk sewing thread. Each spermatozoon starts forming at the outer edge of the tubule.

At first it looks very much like any ordinary body cell, but as it progresses, tail first, toward the hollow interior of the tubule it gradually assumes its familiar tadpole shape.

From the seminiferous tubule the developing sperm cell goes to the epididymis, an eighteen-foot coiled tube whose name, "that which lies on the twins," accurately describes its anatomical location.

In man the evolution of the sex cells in the seminiferous tubules takes forty-eight days. Then the spermatozoa spend another twelve days in the epididymis. From there they pass quickly through the *vas deferens,* the upper end of the epididymis, which terminates in the seminal vesicle.

Now the sperm are ready for ejaculation. At the appropriate time they are mixed with seminal fluid manufactured by the prostate and other accessory sex glands. The seminal fluid contains nutrients and enzymes that have been likened to spark plugs, for they put the sperm "in motion."

Only a very few of the prodigious number of sperm cells that enter the female tract reach their final destination. In the rabbit, for instance, only 2,000,000 of the 200,000,000 sperm ejaculated succeed in passing through the cervical canal and reaching the uterus. By then many cells start to disintegrate or get lost. Only 5,000 sperm cells manage to enter the oviducts where fertilization takes place.

The function of the testes, like that of the ovaries, is ruled by hormones. The principal male sex hormone, testosterone, is produced by the testes. As in the female, local hormone production is masterminded by hormones that go by the collective name of gonadotropins and are identical for both sexes. At puberty the follicle-stimulating hormone (FSH) and the lutenizing hormone (LH) initiate spermatogenesis as well as testosterone production; the latter leads to sexual maturation and the development of secondary male sex characteristics.

When testosterone was first isolated in 1931, it was hoped that it would remedy male infertility, which is responsible for one-third of all childless marriages.

However, it became quickly apparent that testosterone did not help the sterile. Quite to the contrary, it stopped spermatogenesis. This unexpected result was caused by the suppression of gonadotropin production by the pituitary via the seesaw effect that has been so effectively exploited in female contraception.

Even though testosterone was thus useless for its intended purpose, scientists thought they were on the road to finding the first male pill. Unfortunately, things did not work out that way. Testosterone is a tricky substance, and its administration has many side effects. Like natural progesterone, it must be injected, and furthermore, there is some indication that it increases male aggressiveness beyond a stage that is desired by either men or women. In some men it also causes a constant erection.

Though some scientists are still attempting to turn testosterone into a useful antifertility agent, perhaps by combining it with estrogen or with a progesteronelike drug, other investigators are concentrating on developing a nonsteroid male pill. This seems to be easier said than done. Several potential male pills have come and gone over the past years. One of the most noteworthy was an amebicide drug that when taken by mouth inhibited spermatogenesis. Its effect was completely reversible. When the drug was discontinued, sperm counts returned to normal levels within a couple of weeks. Birthcontrollers were happy. Unfortunately, the pill had been tested on volunteer convicts who, by necessity, were complete teetotalers. When the first free-living volunteer drank so much as a glass of beer he had severe convulsions, and the drug had to be shelved.

Spermatogenesis can also be halted by drugs that interfere with rapidly dividing cells. Such agents include the nitrogen mustards and other anticancer drugs. (Cancer cells, like the cells that are precursors of spermatozoa, divide at a very rapid rate.) All anticancer drugs tested so far have proven much too toxic to be used on a regular basis by healthy men.

Recently those involved in attempting to develop a male pill have come to the conclusion that it would be much more desirable to interfere with a very late stage of sperm development.

An almost natural "late stage" at which one could interfere with the sperm cells is during their passage through the epididymis. Dr. J. Michael Bedford of Cornell University Medical School, who has been investigating spermatogenesis for a number of years, feels that "disarming" sperm cells at that point in their development would be akin to producing cars without spark plugs.

At present Dr. Bedford is investigating the epididymal maturation rate of various animals. The differences between species he has observed so far are striking. Frogs produce completely mature sperm in their testes. Rabbits and hamsters do not, and the capacity of their sperm to impregnate the females varies by 64 percent according to whether the sample is removed from the testes end of the epididymis or the vas end.

Nobody yet knows exactly where human sperm matures. There is hope that a drug which specifically acts on the epididymis may indeed become the elusive male pill. Since the epididymis requires some androgen to function properly, an antiandrogen drug is a likely male antifertility agent.

Search for an effective male pill is one of the chief activities of Dr. R. J. Ericsson, a young American pharmaceutical chemist who now works for the Schering A. G. drug firm in Berlin, West Germany.

As of the latest count Dr. Ericsson has tested seven thousand preselected chemicals for their potential use as a male antifertility agent. Of these eighty-nine had a definite contraceptive effect. The most promising belonged to the chlorohydrin family, and the star was a substance called alpha-chlorohydrin.

When tested in rats it apparently incapacitated the sperm during the maturation process in the epididymis. The exact way in which incapacitation takes place is not yet known. When examined under the microscope, the ejaculated sperm looked completely normal. Furthermore, the sterilizing effect was only temporary; once the drug was discontinued, the test males sired normal litters.

But alpha-chlorohydrin was not to be a useful male pill. Like other potential candidates, it simply is too toxic to be used on a regular basis. Dr. Ericsson's efforts, however, were not wasted. Since alpha-chlorohydrin is an ideal antifertility compound for rats, mankind is about to have a very effective rat-control agent.

Apart from bringing relief to the many still living in rat-infested slums, the agent can be used to further the understanding of spermatogenesis and maturation of sperm at the level of the epididymis.

Much effort is being expended to determine what happens to the sperm when it reaches the female. In some species, if not in all, the sperm must reside for a number of hours in the friendly estrogen-loaded female tract. Only then is it capable of fertilizing the ovum. This step is called capacitation.

Modification of the hormonal environment of the vagina is a likely point at which human fertility could be interfered with. Fertilization does not take place in a progestin-dominated environment.

The mini-pill, which has just been marketed in the United States, supplies the female with enough progestin to prevent fertilization, but not enough to prevent ovulation and menstruation. It is believed to work because it keeps the female tract in its progestin-loaded infertile state.

Some scientists have suggested that contraception could be achieved by sneaking some progestins into the seminal vesicle where the sperm is stored prior to ejaculation.

Another point of control might be the swimming rate of the spermatozoon. The speed at which it travels again depends on the hormonal climate of the female tract. According to Dr. Bedford, sperm cells seem to move rapidly, "like cars along a turnpike," when the female is near ovulation. At other times of the month, when progestin is dominant, the mucus that guards the entrance to the cervix becomes almost impenetrable. Excess progestin, as in the mini-pill, again seems to be a possible means of control.

Scientists are also interfering with the speed at which the fertilized ovum, or zygote, travels through the fallopian tubes. Normally this journey takes several days, and the zygote arrives in the uterus at the precise moment the latter is prepared for nidation. Tubal transport again is regulated by the twin female hormones. Estrogens, in animals at least, speed up tubal transport to such an extent that the zygote fails to nidate. When administered postcoitally and in large amounts, estrogens have effectively prevented the impregnation of a colony of monkeys that normally had a pregnancy rate of 70 percent. Estrogens, including the synthetic diethylstilbestrol, are the chief constituent of the "morning after" pill, but they cause such severe side effects that they should be used only in an emergency. Work on other types of postcoital pills is underway.

Instead of working on a chemical substance that halts spermatogenesis, maturation, or capacitation, some researchers are trying to develop a sort of vaccine that interferes with sperm production. Here again there is more than one approach. The immunological agent could be directed against either the hormones that regulate spermatogenesis or those that control oogenesis. A woman could be immunized against her husband's sperm, or spermatogenesis could be halted, as shown in animal experiments, by injecting a small amount of testicular extract.

Practically all reversible methods of birth control involve some unknown, long-term physiological risk, a certain percentage of failures, and/or attention at inconvenient times. This is why some people are opting for permanent sterility. Voluntary sterilization of both men and women has become much more popular. Last year one million men underwent this operation in the United States alone.

Today the sterilization of men has become a relatively easy operation, one that does not even involve hospitalization. The procedure is called a vasectomy because it involves severance (cutting) of the vas deferens—the upper end of the epididymis.

The great advantage of a vasectomy is that it does not interfere with any essential physiological process. Hormone manufacture continues as usual, as does the production of mature sperm cells and seminal fluid. The only difference is that the ejaculate no longer contains any sperm.

Because of their great concern for the environment and the population explosion, several well-known persons have had vasectomies. They include Paul Ehrlich, author of *The Population Bomb,* and Jim Bouton, the baseball star and sports commentator.

Most of those who have undergone vasectomies are willing to testify that the procedure does not interfere with their sex drive, and some report that it has given them a new sense of freedom.

It must be understood that a vasectomy should be considered irreversible, even though some surgeons are quite skillful at reconnecting the disconnected vas. The development of sperm banks in which a man can store some of his potential progeny might turn out to be a safeguard for those who feel they might change their minds. At present, however, there is the possibility that sperm which have been stored for a long time may give rise to a high number of malformed offspring.

Several laboratories are in the process of developing reversible vasectomies. One possibility might be the use of a silastic (plastic) thread that when threaded into the vas can act as an effective barrier. One of the attractive features of this method is that the thread can be inserted by nonphysician personnel. Limited field trials, however, have shown the method to be unsuitable so far.

Dr. Hans Zinsser of Columbia Presbyterian Medical Center has blocked the vas temporarily by injecting it with a mixture of liquid silicone and a chemical that will accelerate the solidification process. Once in place, the liquid turns into a solid plug, which dissolves within six to eight months. This method is now in the animal-testing stage.

Another approach to reversible vasectomies involves tiny gold microvalves developed by bioengineer Louis Bucalo. These "phasers" can be implanted by a urologist in the vas, under local anesthesia, within a matter of half an hour. Once installed, they can rapidly be switched on and off by a doctor, again under local anesthesia. Phasers are presently being tested in some thirty volunteers, all of whom had previously opted for vasectomies.

According to the statistics of the Association for Voluntary Sterilization, there also has been an upswing in female sterilizations. Since the fallopian tubes are deeply imbedded in the abdominal cavity, the procedure is more complex. Until recently "tubal ligation," as the operation is called, involved total anesthesia and several days of hospitalization.

A new procedure, pioneered by Dr. Clifford R. Wheeless of Johns Hopkins Hospital in Baltimore, can be done on an outpatient basis. Some doctors, however, prefer to hospitalize their patients overnight.

The operation is nicknamed "Band-Aid" or "belly button" surgery because it involves a small incision below the navel. The latter is pasted over, after surgery, with a narrow bandage.

The instrument used for the operation is a laparoscope, a long tube the size of a fountain pen, equipped with an eyepiece, a light, and something that can best be described as a pair of electrified tweezers.

After the instrument is inserted in the abdominal cavity through the small incision, the physician "looks" for the tubes. Once located, each oviduct is snipped and sealed electrically.

Tubal ligations, like vasectomies, are still irreversible, but some physicians, including Dr. Martin Clyman of Mount Sinai Medical Center in New York City, are experimenting with reversible methods. Dr. Clyman has developed a bobby-pin-like clip to be slipped on each tube. Theoretically the clip could be removed later when the woman wanted to resume her fertility.

The difficulty of reversibility in both men and women is that when tied or blocked, both the vas and the tubes tend to form natural adhesions that are almost impossible to remove by present-day surgical techniques.

10
Abortion

On January 23, 1973, the Supreme Court of the United States ruled that abortion, when carried out during the first three months of pregnancy, is a private matter between the pregnant woman and her physician.

Thus ended one of the most hotly debated, emotionally charged issues that the country had faced in recent years.

The Supreme Court resolved the issue on purely legal grounds. In the majority opinion, written by Justice Harry A. Blackmun, the Court stated:

We need not resolve the difficult question of when life begins. When those trained in the respective disciplines of medicine, philosophy and theology are unable to arrive at any consensus, the judiciary, at this point in the development of man's knowledge, is not in a position to speculate as to the answer.

The unborn have never been recognized in the law as persons in the whole sense.

With respect to the state's important and legitimate interest in the health of the mother, the "compelling" point in the light of present medical knowledge, is at approximately the end of the first trimester. This is so because of the now established medical fact that until the end of the first trimester mortality in abortion is less than mortality in normal childbirth.

It is also believed by many observers that the Court chose the end of the first trimester as a cut-off date (regulation of abortion after that date is left to the jurisdiction of the states) because prior to this time the fetus does not have the capability of a meaningful life outside the mother's womb.

The abortion question reached the Supreme Court since all states (as well as almost all foreign countries) now have laws regulating abortion. Abortion is the only medical procedure treated specifically by law. This was not always so. In England it became a crime only in 1803. For a while after that there was a distinction between abortions that took place before the fetus had moved or "quickened"—this offense carried a sentence of fourteen years of indentured servitude—or a late abortion, which was punishable by hanging.

Abortions, or attempts at abortion, were probably common among prehistoric people. A Chinese medical text, thought to have been written 4,600 years ago by Emperor Shun Nung, recommended a mercury potion as an abortifacient (abortion-inducing drug), and the Ebers papyrus (1550 B.C.) states that a concoction made of "dates, onions, and the fruit of the acanthus, crushed with honey and applied to the vulva," would induce abortion. The physicians of ancient Arabia advised "those who abhor pregnancy" to take prolonged baths and to "increase the respiratory effort, so that the fetus is deprived of fresh air and consequently dies." The Romans, always partial to water, recommended soaking in a full tub to which a "decoction of fenugreek, mallow and mugwort" had been added.

More than any other medical procedure, abortion is often self-inflicted. Aside from pure magic, which never did any good, and poisonous chemicals, which often killed both the mother and her unborn child, women often resorted to violent physical means.

Popular ways of getting rid of an unwanted pregnancy included jumping, hitting the belly of the woman with a big stick, or having a third party jump on her stomach.

A more effective way of inducing an abortion was the introduc-

112

"Messrs. Editors,—As a new phase of quack advertising has of late presented itself, it may be proper to give it a little consideration. I refer to the practice of advertising drugs for *producing abortion.* These advertisements have become so villainously common that one can hardly find a weekly newspaper whose columns are free from the nuisance; which, while they recommend abortions in an indirect manner, do not fail to impress upon the minds of the public that miscarriage can be produced, certainly and safely, with drugs! The following will serve as a specimen of the whole class. It is taken from a paper published and extensively circulated in Northern Ohio:—

"'Ladies in want of a pleasant and safe remedy for irregularities, obstructions &c., should use Dr. Miller's Female Monthly Powders. It has been said that these powders will produce miscarriage. Without admitting the truth of this assertion, I must confess that it is the inevitable consequence of their use during the early months of pregnancy. Therefore ladies who desire an increase of family should not use them. If after this caution any lady in a certain situation should use them, she must hold herself responsible for the abortion which will surely follow. Price $5. Sent by mail to any part of the country.'

"Such notices cannot fail to do evil by familiarizing the public with the idea that abortion may be produced whenever one does not desire an increase of family, and its strange that editors and publishers, who claim to be the guardians of the public health and morals, should thus aid in sowing broadcast the seeds of grossest immorality, crime and suffering, and in robbing the public of money and health.

A roundabout way of advertising an abortifacient, published in the *Boston Medical and Surgical Journal* in 1858.

tion of a foreign body into the uterus. Peeled branches of slippery elm were popular in Europe. These sticks often swelled in the womb and caused the uterus to contract and attempt to expel the fetus.

A variant of the slippery elm is still used in South America today. It consists of a kind of algae that swells when slipped into the womb. This often induces an abortion. Knitting needles and other sharp instruments are also popular.

The number of self-induced and nonprofessional abortions was particularly high in Chile, a country that, like most of South America, has a very high birth rate. By the mid-1960's the number of abortions performed annually had reached epidemic proportions, and in 1966, 57,000 patients with incomplete or "botched" abortions had to be admitted to hospitals. These cases occupied a large share of all available maternity beds. Deaths as a result of abortion accounted for 40 percent of all "maternal deaths."

These staggering figures galvanized the Chilean government into action. Birth-control clinics were established in all of Santiago's public hospitals. Many private institutions, including the Catholic University, followed suit.

Women, especially those hospitalized after an abortion, were offered a choice of birth-control methods. Most women opted for the IUD, and fewest for the rhythm method.

Today the birth rate of Chile, which has the most active birth-control program in all of South America, has dropped. So far, however, there has been no change in the ratio of births to abortions. Though difficult to prove, some sociologists attribute this to the fact that the birth-control propaganda that accompanies the official antiabortion policy has spread down to the least-educated segment of the population. Ordinarily, many women belonging to this group would have carried their unwanted babies to term. Now, as a first step, they resort to the most primitive method of birth control available: abortion. In due time these women too will come to the birth-control centers, but this unexpected development is an example of the complexity and unpredictability of social problems.

Even though death resulting from self-induced abortions motivated Margaret Sanger and Alan Guttmacher to devote their lives to birth control, abortion performed early in the course of pregnancy is a safe medical procedure provided current techniques are used. Such interventions are also not limited to the termination of unwanted pregnancy. They are often used in gynecology to complete a spontaneous miscarriage.

Abortions done for whatever reason must be carried out under conditions approximating the proverbial "operating room cleanliness." The reason that today's kitchentable abortionist causes less harm than his predecessor did, is that he usually gives his client a whopping dose of antibiotics, which make short shrift of the galloping uterine infections, or "childbed fevers," that killed so many women in the past.

When done during the first thirteen weeks of pregnancy, an abortion is a minor procedure. Until a few years ago the classic technique was the D and C, an operation that we have already encountered in Dr. Graefenberg's office in Berlin.

D and C's are, however, time-consuming and far from easy to do. In the late 1960's a "new" method appeared on the medical horizon, and it is rapidly becoming the standard procedure. As is so often the case, it is not really all that new. The aspiration technique, or vacuum abortion, was devised by a Soviet physician in 1927, but was not used until its revival in China a little more than ten years ago. From there it spread to Eastern Europe, Russia, Great Britain, and Japan. Today it is widely used in the United States.

The aspiration technique involves sucking out of the uterus its soft, loosely attached contents. The apparatus used is so simple that almost anyone can assemble it. The most complicated component is a small vacuum pump. The rest consists of glass bottles and plastic tubes. What is even more important, abortion by aspiration is a walkaway office procedure, which can be done by nonphysician personnel.

Women have always wished for a pill that would undo unwanted pregnancies. Such medications are hard to come by because the life of the mother and that of her unborn child are so intimately linked that what is poison for one is usually also poison for the other. It is only as a last resort, and often even not then, that the body is willing to give up its contribution to the survival of the species.

The low success rate of drugs alleged to induce abortion did not deter everybody. Dr. Christopher Tietze, who was involved in the early testing of the IUD and is a world authority on abortion, recalls that when he was a medical student in Vienna some thirty-five years ago women used to swallow phosphorus-containing matches to induce abortion. The practice was so common that medical students working at the morgue were instructed to determine whether women who died of phosphorus poisoning had been pregnant. Strong cathartics were also widely used in attempts to induce abortion.

Scientists are still hunting for an effective abortifacient. Prime candidates are members of the prostaglandin family—a still poorly understood group of hormonelike compounds. Very small amounts of two prostaglandins cause the uterus to contract. When injected directly into the amniotic fluid that surrounds the embryo, they are used to induce abortion during the second trimester of pregnancy.

Some prostaglandins can induce abortions when given early during pregnancy, but even when successful, they cause such severe cramps and other side effects that they are not useful.

Drug companies are presently trying to develop compounds that ressemble to prostaglandins as far as their abortifacient properties are concerned, but which lack their unpleasant side effects.

It has been amply proven in Japan and in some of the Eastern European countries that free availability of abortion can result in halting or even in decreasing a rising birth rate. No government, however, has ever advocated it to be the mainstay of its contraceptive effort. Apart from moral considerations, abortions, especially when repeated frequently, involve a certain risk of complications. Even when "cheap," they are always more expensive than contraception.

The number of legal and illegal abortions performed each year throughout the world indicates that there is a need to improve contraception and to make whatever contraceptive techniques exist freely available and known to all those in need.

Abortion should primarily be a back-up procedure for birth control. The reason is quite simple. Women who do not have easy access to abortion will usually insist on a very safe method of contraception. One such method is the Pill. It is practically foolproof, yet the continuous intake of high doses of hormones is looked on with misgiving by some members of the medical profession.

It is probably more desirable from a medical point of view to use a low-dose pill or a mechanical device like the IUD or diaphragm, which may be less than 100 percent effective but which have the great advantage of not interfering with the delicate physiological balance of the body.

Some experts believe that the liberalized abortion law may have a favorable impact on decreasing teen-age pregnancy. Communities faced with the alternative of having to terminate pregnancies in young adults may find it more desirable to provide contraceptive measures.

Failure to use birth control was responsible for the unwanted pregnancies of 66 percent of 144 women who underwent legal abortions in one Boston hospital between 1968 and 1970. In a follow-up questionnaire they attributed their pregnancies to lack of birth-control information and sex education.

Voluntary abortion has usually been considered to be a good thing from the mother's point of view. There is however, some considerable data showing that unwanted children suffer too. In Sweden 120 children born to women who were denied therapeutic

116

abortions were studied for twenty years. The rate of crime, antisocial behavior, psychiatric illness, and public dependence of this group was twice as high as that occurring in a comparable group of wanted children.

At a time when abortion has become such a controversial issue, it might be well to remember that many religions do not consider that the fetus has a soul of its own until some time after conception or even until the child is born. Abortion is tolerated by the Shinto, Moslem, and Buddhist religions, and even the Roman Catholic Church changed its mind on the matter repeatedly during its long history.

In spite of severe legal restrictions in the past, most women seemed to be able to muster the services of an abortionist if they so desired and had enough money. It has been estimated that in recent years one million abortions were performed annually in the United States.

Abortion in the states then had a status similar to the sale of alcoholic beverages during the prohibition of the 1920's. For even though nobody ever approved of alcoholism, and some religions forbid the consumption of liquor altogether, legal prohibition did not really profit anyone but the bootleggers.

The Supreme Court ruling on abortion has, one hopes, put an end to the crime and profit associated with abortion. Now the procedure is purely a private matter, which each woman or couple can decide according to their religious and moral beliefs.

11

New Developments in Contraception

In medicine one discovery usually leads to other closely related ones. It took centuries to find vaccines with which to ward off infectious diseases. Today there are dozens of different vaccines. The same is true of antibiotics, the first of which was developed a short thirty years ago; of vitamins, first proven essential at the turn of this century; and of artificial joints. A good "total hip" joint was only developed in England during the 1960's, yet by 1980 doctors hope to have man-made finger joints, knees, elbows, and even wrists.

Such a pattern should also apply to new methods of contraception. As a topic of scientific investigation, the subject was practically nonexistent until Margaret Sanger visited with Gregory Pincus in the early 1950's. Contraceptive and reproductive research has become highly respectable since, and even though it still does not receive the attention it deserves, people today have a wide choice of birth-control methods. More are to be released soon.

Few of these are entirely new. Most female oral contraceptive methods still rely on interference with the two sex hormones, estrogens and progesterone. But whereas the early editions of the pill contained as much as 9 mg of progestin per pill, the modern versions contain but 0.5 mg. This dramatically reduces side effects and also lessens the long-term risk that may be associated with hormones. Dosage continues to be reduced, especially in view of the fact that progestin, when taken on a regular round-the-month basis, apparently prevents conception without interfering with ovulation. In early clinical trials women taking such mini-pills, as the preparation is appropriately called, continued to menstruate regularly. Though scientists are still investigating why the mini-pill is effective, they suspect that it works by influencing the speed at which either the ovum or the sperm or both travel through the female reproductive tract.

For a while it had looked as if the mini-pill would turn out to be the mainstay of the next generation of oral contraceptives, but recently these hopes have been shattered. Women on the mini-pill have considerably more menstrual irregularities and a great many more unwanted pregnancies than women taking the standard pill.

The need to swallow a pill on a daily basis for years on end is not only a burden but results in numerous "contraceptive failures." Birthcontrollers are developing means through which they can deliver hormones on a continuous basis from a reservoir stored within the body itself.

Such delivery systems would also benefit diabetics and other persons whose health rests on taking medication on a daily basis. Dr. Sheldon Segal, director of the Biomedical Division of the Population Council in New York, has been working for a number of years with silastic capsules filled with progestin. The capsules are small enough so that they can be "injected" under the skin by means of a hypodermic needle. Once in place and surrounded by the moisture of the body, the silastic membrane acts like a fine sieve through which tiny amounts of progestin pass at a continuous rate. The silastic capsules can be filled with enough progestin to provide contraception for up to fifteen months. They also can be removed at will by a physician. The method is now in the advanced stages of clinical testing, and the results are promising.

Some chemicals, by their very nature, are released very slowly from the site at which they have been injected. This in effect also reduces the number of times a year that a woman has to think "contraception."

119

Among this type of contraceptives the most widely studied substance is the progestin medroxyprogesterone acetate. It needs to be injected only every three to six months, has already been tried on several thousand women, and is a very effective antifertility compound.

At the chosen dosage levels, the drug has, however, many unpleasant side effects, and it takes months, if not years, after discontinuation for a woman to resume her regular menstrual pattern. Much more research will have to be done before the preparation can become a useful contraceptive.

The same substance has already been used with a minimum of side effects in an open silastic ring that is inserted into the vagina much like a diaphragm. The principle involved in the slow release of the chemical substance is much the same as that used in Dr. Segal's silastic capsule. Small amounts of the antifertility compound escape at a constant rate, and conception is effectively prevented by inhibition of ovulation resulting from the action of the progestin on the pituitary, as in the oral contraceptive pill. The ring is left in place for three weeks at a time. A new ring is inserted after menstruation.

Intrauterine devices filled with progestins are just now beginning to be clinically tested. So far it is impossible to decide whether such progestin-filled IUD's are superior to plain, purely mechanical models.

Contraceptive research is also zeroing in on the corpus luteum. In 1907, long before progesterone itself had been identified, the corpus luteum had been proven essential to maintain pregnancy.

Today several research scientists are attempting to find chemical substances that specifically interfere with the corpus luteum. It is hoped that such luteolytic, or "corpus lutenum dissolving," compounds would effectively prevent the implantation of the fertilized ovum.

Instead of silencing the corpus luteum by chemical means, some researchers are attempting to keep it functioning for more than its natural lifespan of two weeks. This would correspond to the state of pseudopregnancy induced by the progestins of the Pill except that the progestational hormone would be supplied by the woman herself.

Dr. Segal speculates that a compound which could keep the corpus luteum alive could be so administered that a woman would ovulate only three to four times a year instead of the usual twelve.

Ancient and primitive societies often relied on the contraceptive power of various sticky salves introduced into the vagina before intercourse. Indeed, acid and alkaline preparations do inactivate some of the sperm, and the salves offer a moderately effective mechanical barrier.

A concentrated search for effective spermicidal chemicals dates from the turn of the century. Today the base of most jellies consists of glycerine and starch and a vegetable gum. A mild acid is added to the jellies or creams that are supposed to be used in conjunction with both the diaphragm and condom. When used on their own, such preparations are rather ineffectual.

Recently a more effective spermicide—which goes by the jaw-breaking name of nonylphenoxypolyethoxyethanol (nony-g for short)—has appeared on the market. It is usually incorporated into aerosol vaginal foams that are moderately effective. As with other contraceptives, researchers promise progress. According to Dr. Irving Scheer of Ortho Pharmaceutical Company, which pioneered the diaphragm in the United States forty years ago, spermicide foams are "rapidly becoming the most popular form of vaginal contraception."

Diaphragms inspected during their manufacture.

Though these are still in the drawing-board stage, Dr. Scheer envisions "chemical agents that will provide effective protection for 24 hours." If these could be coupled with a new type of delivery system that needs only to be inserted on a weekly or monthly basis, vaginal contraception could effectively compete with other methods of fertility control.

The classic IUD, which was greeted enthusiastically fifteen years ago, caused many more unpleasant side effects than had been anticipated. Since by their very nature intrauterine devices are one of the most attractive methods of contraception, scientists have continued to search for better models. The primary objective was to reduce their size. This, scientists felt, would eliminate the bleeding and severe cramps that are the primary reasons for discontinuation in some users. Less contact with the walls of the uterus would probably also reduce the involuntary contractions that often lead to spontaneous expulsion.

According to Dr. Howard J. Tatum of the Population Council, this manner of reasoning proved correct. Smaller IUD's had fewer side effects. Unfortunately, they also were responsible for a great many more contraceptive failures.

While Tatum was experimenting with a small IUD, his colleague Dr. Jaime Zipper of Santiago, Chile, was using the same "T" with the addition of a thin copper wire.

Using copper instead of gold or silver as Graefenberg had in the early days was not a matter of economy. Copper has proved to have remarkable antifertility properties in animals, like rabbits and rats, with bifurcated uteri. When Dr. Tatum placed a small amount of copper in one of the horns of the uterus, the animals regularly conceived in the other horn. The copper did not cause permanent infertility. When the metal was switched to the other horn, the animals obliged by conceiving in the unprotected half of the uterus.

The Cu-7 IUD (Cu is chemical shorthand for copper) and its companion the copper T-200 have proved very successful when tested in large-scale clinical trials, and unlike their classic "big brothers," can be used by women whose uteri have not previously been stretched by childbearing.

For a long time scientists interested in contraception have been saying that the problems would be much simpler if ovulation could be predicted with any degree of accuracy. Such a test would be

122

particularly important for women who want to practice the rhythm method for religious reasons.

Women are the only females in which ovulation is, so to speak, "silent" and unassociated with a characteristic mating behavior. This lack of obvious signals was responsible for the fact that it was not until the 1930's that scientists could pinpoint the fact that ovulation occurred midway between menstrual cycles, and not, as had been assumed, at menstruation.

No biological phenomenon, especially when it follows such a rigid rhythmical pattern, can be completely hidden, and ovulation in the human female is accompanied by certain detectable changes.

Dr. Gerald Oster and his group at Mount Sinai School of Medicine in New York are determined to develop a useful test by which a woman can predict that she will ovulate within a matter of two to three days—the time prior to ovulation during which she must abstain from intercourse if she wants to avoid pregnancy.

It is known that ovulation is accompanied by a slight but reliable increase in basal body temperature. This sign is, however, useless because it does not precede ovulation.

Dr. Oster is presently developing an ovulation test based on the fact that saliva changes with the estrogen level of the blood. The original idea for the test was derived from the observation that there is considerable difference in the appearance of the salivary glands of male and female rats. However, when the ovaries of the females were removed surgically, the salivary glands of the females started to resemble those of the males.

An investigation of the saliva of women showed that it undergoes chemical changes that closely parallel those observed in the cervical mucus. The consistency (viscosity) of both fluids decreases markedly when the estrogen level is near its maximum. This occurs exactly two days before ovulation.

At present Dr. Oster can determine ovulation by means of his saliva test in the laboratory, but this is hardly of practical use to the average woman. A "spit test" based on color reaction is what is needed.

Accurate means of predicting ovulation are as important for the infertile as for the overfertile. It has been noted that couples with rather low fertility conceive more readily when intercourse is adjusted to ovulation time.

Since parents often continue to reproduce until they have at least one child of each sex, it would be very important, from a contraceptive point of view, to develop a method that could be used to choose the sex of one's progeny. There is a small difference in the weight and speed of travel of "male" and "female" sperm, but as of now there is no sure way in which these can be exploited.

Even if contraceptive methods continue to be improved, there will always be mishaps and failures. Dr. Harvey Kaplan of Los Angeles has developed a method by which a possible pregnancy can be terminated within days after the woman has missed her period.

Menstrual extraction, as this simple office procedure is called, involves the emptying of the uterine cavity by means of a 4 mm plastic tube (cannula) attached to a syringe. One of the advantages of the method is that the cannula is thin enough to pass through the undilated cervical canal. In point of fact, menstrual extraction is simply an early vacuum abortion.

So far, this method has been used for more than five thousand women. It can be used up to seven weeks after the last period, but it is often performed as early as the tenth day after the missed period. Taking the usual variation of a woman's menstrual cycle into consideration, one would expect that intervention at such an early date would often turn out to have been a false alarm. A survey conducted by the National Woman's Health Coalition, a volunteer organization concerned with the health problems of women and children, indicates that the "hunches" of 70 percent of the women who requested and underwent menstrual extraction were correct.

Though undoubtedly effective, there is no data, as of now, that indicates whether the method is harmful when used repeatedly.

An entirely new approach to contraception may involve the hypothalamus, a region in the base of the brain that is connected to the "master gland" by a narrow stalk. The pituitary produces a number of hormones, including FSH and LH, which play a crucial role in reproduction.

It now appears that the release of LH, and probably also of FSH, is controlled by yet another set of chemicals produced by the hypothalamus. These rather simple molecules are called after the hormone whose release they control, for instance, lutenizing-hormone releasing factor, or LRF for short.

Instead of suppressing the production of FSH and LH by artificially supplying the body with progestins and/or estrogens, one could obtain the same effect by suppressing the hypothalamic releasing factors. In practice birthcontrollers envision supplying the body with a chemical molecule similar enough to the natural releasing factor so that it effectively competes with LRF. This theoretically would prevent the release of LH and consequently inhibit the formation of the corpus luteum.

If a similar method of reasoning were applied to the male, LRF would interfere with the production of testosterone.

The whole approach, at present, is only a hopeful possibility, but at a time when there is such an emphasis on the equality of the sexes it is interesting to speculate about a "unisex" birth-control pill.

In spite of all the contraceptive methods that are available today, perfection has not yet been achieved. According to estimates made recently by the Office of Population Research at Princeton University, 44 percent of all births to married women during a five-year period were unplanned, and 15 percent were unwanted. (An "unplanned birth" is one that occurs at an inopportune time, and an "unwanted birth" is one that was never to take place. Neither group of babies necessarily become unloved children, but since overpopulation is a problem today, it would be desirable to postpone—or eliminate—both types of pregnancies.) The large number of abortions, legal or otherwise, that are being performed throughout the world is another indication that problems remain.

Because it is within human nature to forget, take chances, or simply be ignorant of how a method works, even the best contraceptives, by themselves, will not entirely eliminate unplanned and unwanted pregnancies. A wider choice of methods coupled with education would, however, go far in reducing population growth. Yet it is not the whole answer.

What is also needed is the acceptance of the fact that the earth can barely cope with its present population. Tapering off population growth will require a major change of attitude on the part of society as a whole as well as on the part of each individual couple. For each infant ultimately is the result of a decision made by two people only.

12
There Was an Old Woman Who Lived in a Shoe

Fecundity and Prosperity

In ancient times, people were few but wealthy and without strife. People at present think that five sons are not too many, and each son has five sons also and before the death of the grandfather there are already twenty-five descendents. Therefore people are more and wealth is less; they work hard and receive little. The life of a nation depends upon people having enough food, not upon the number of people.

Han Fei-Tzu (Chou Dynasty, circa 500 b.c.)

Emperor Han Fei-Tzu's view of population is an exception. Throughout history, practically all religious and secular authorities believed that the wealth and well-being of their nation were closely related to a growing population.

During the time mankind struggled with a high death rate, such an attitude was reasonable to ensure survival of the species. A look at the many small gravestones that still can be found in old cemeteries is proof enough that a large number of children did not grow to adulthood. Childbearing itself was a great hazard, and it was common for a husband to bury several wives before he himself died at a relatively young age.

126

An old-fashioned agricultural society also profited from extra farm hands, and when industry first came into being it put child labor to good use.

The need for a high birth rate has long disappeared, but society still looks favorably upon the prolific. In the United States, for example, large families have a decided tax advantage over small families, and single persons are heavily discriminated against by existing tax laws. In many other countries motherhood is actually subsidized.

In America, as elsewhere, childbearing is greeted with approval. A look at the popular television soap operas indicates that the country is enthralled by large families, especially when they are poor and cope in spite of a long string of misfortunes. Single males and childless couples are considered selfish; single women are an object of pity and contempt.

It had always been assumed that provided adequate methods of birth control were available, family size would be a matter of free individual choice. Sociological research indicates that fashion and economic considerations play a major role.

The dearth of births that accompanied the Depression of the 1930's proved that people manage to have fewer children when they choose to, even when they must rely on uncertain methods of contraception such as withdrawal, condoms, and abortions. The baby boom of the post-World War II years and the smaller families of the early 1970's again indicate that the birth rate is as sensitive an indicator of the "social climate" as the stock market is of the economy.

The fact that trends in population growth are related to social factors is illustrated by the fertility behavior of some societies that either sanctioned contraception or in which social pressures favored small families.

Such an example is the fertility control exercised in Arab countries during the Middle Ages. This subject was recently examined from available records by Basim Mussalam, a graduate student of Harvard University's Center for Population Studies. Withdrawal and other primitive methods of birth control were acceptable in Islam, on both legal and religious grounds, for several reasons—the desire to preserve a woman's beauty and physical appeal, the fear for a woman's life from the danger of childbearing, the fear of economic hardship resulting from large family size, and the protection of oneself from wrongdoing in the struggle to earn more money so as to care for a larger family. Practicing contraception in order to avoid begetting daughters was not acceptable.

During the Middle Ages, and contrary to present-day customs, most Islamic philosophers felt that both marriage partners must agree to the practice of contraception.

Since the Near East as well as Europe was subject to such familiar population checks as pestilence, high infant mortality, and famine, Dr. Mussalam believes that the tolerant attitude toward contraception was responsible for the fact that the population of Syria and Egypt declined drastically from the eleventh to the nineteenth century, while that of Western Europe kept rising.

Even though birthcontrollers, social workers, and others have long been concerned with the size of the individual family and the effect of constant childbearing on the health of the mother, few until recently were alarmed by the impact of population growth on the country as a whole.

This view has changed radically in the past decades. Population problems have ceased to be the sole concern of intellectuals or prophets of gloom like Thomas Malthus, but have become a topic of prime importance to heads of state as varied as President Richard M. Nixon, Chairman Mao Tse-tung, and Prime Minister Indira Gandhi.

The problems faced by the countries of these three statesmen are very different. Yet rich nations as well as poor are beginning to face the fact that in order to maintain or improve their standard of living, they must put a lid on their mushrooming numbers.

Both President Johnson and President Nixon voiced concern about population matters in the United States. In 1969 President Nixon appointed a special Commission on Population Growth and the American Future, which was to make recommendations on the official population policy to be followed by the United States, for, as the President stated: "One of the most serious challenges to human destiny in the last third of this century will be the growth of the population. Whether man's response to that challenge will be cause for pride or for despair in the year 2000 will depend very much on what we do today."

The chairman of the commission was John D. Rockefeller III, who was hardly a newcomer to the problem, since he had founded the Population Council in 1952. The twenty-three other commissioners included housewives, physicians, congressmen, and economists.

The commission relied heavily on data supplied by outside experts. During the two years of its existence, it listened to more than a hundred witnesses and initiated a hundred independent research projects.

The commission began by examining the phenomenal growth of the population in the United States during its brief history. America has always assumed that "bigger is better." As the commission stated in the opening lines of its report:

Population growth has frequently been regarded as a measure of our progress. If that were ever the case, it is not now. There is hardly any social problem confronting this nation whose solution would be easier if our population were larger. Even now, the dreams of too many Americans are not being realized; others are being fulfilled at too high a cost. Accordingly, this Commission has concluded that our country can no longer afford the uncritical acceptance of "more is better."

Demographic data is usually so abstract that it loses much of its meaning for nonprofessional audiences. The commission resolved this difficulty by projecting the future population growth in the United States in terms of a two-child versus a three-child family.

They also emphasized that even though there has been a recent leveling off of the birth rate in the United States, we will live for a long time with the consequences of the recent high birth rates.

The commission wrote:

The postwar baby boom is over, but those born during the boom period are still very much with us. As they move off the college campus or leave their parents' homes, we can expect a 33-percent jump in annual household formation by the end of this decade. . . .
Between 1950 and 1960 the number of households grew at a relatively steady rate of around 900,000 per year, after that the rate began to climb, and last year we added well over a million households. Our research shows that the rate will increase to almost 1.5 million households, added each year, by the end of the seventies, and will remain at that level until about 1985. . . . Along with increased housing demands will come greater demands for employment. . . . The boom generation will continue to exert a heavy impact on our society as they move up the age ladder. The impact will be felt in housing, recreation, crime, medical care, and finally on our retirement system. Today we have an estimated 20 million senior citizens. About 50 years from now we will have . . . about twice as many.

The report concluded:

In sum, it should be evident that, even if the recent unexpected drop in the birth rate should develop into a sustained trend, there is little cause for complacency. Whether we see it or not—whether we like it or not—we are in for a long period of growth, and we had best prepare for it.

When John D. Rockefeller III submitted the final report of the Commission on Population Growth and the American Future to the President and Congress, he summarized its findings by saying:

After two years of concentrated effort, we have concluded that, in the long run, no substantial benefits will result from further growth of the Nation's population, rather that the gradual stabilization of our population would contribute significantly to the Nation's ability to solve its problems. We have looked for, and have not found, any convincing economic argument for continued population growth. The health of the country does not depend on it, nor does the vitality of business nor the welfare of the average person.

The commission did not limit itself to analyzing the problem. It examined the existing social structures of the land and singled out certain attitudes and behavior patterns that must be changed if America is going to alter its traditional "legacy of growth." The final report contains sixty-two major recommendations to be implemented at the federal, state, and local levels.

Foremost among these is education of the citizens at all levels. Even today, few people realize that population is a problem as important as health, food, politics, and money and that ignorance about the most basic facts is widespread. As a subject taught in high school or even at the college level, demography—the study of population—is often neglected. Only half of 537 accredited four-year colleges now offer a course in the subject, and only a very few young people questioned could estimate the size of the population of the United States or that of the world with accuracy.

Knowing about population at a national level is not enough. A modification of the social pressures that make it almost imperative for married couples to become parents is vitally important.

The commission questions the current attitude in a gentle way and suggests that parenthood is perhaps not essential to happiness. "We tend to overlook the fact," the commission states, "that we are not all equally suited for parenthood any more than we are for teaching school or playing sports. Matters of temperament, age, health, and competing interests, to mention a few, are considerations in determining whether or not to have children."

Perhaps to discourage excess childbearing, the commission reviewed the staggering cost of children. A first child from birth until after college costs a middle-class family about $100,000. This figure does not include schooling and other costs borne by the nation as a whole.

The commission believes that much of the educational effort should be directed at changing the status of women. It placed special emphasis on the elimination of adolescent pregnancy. In 1968, 17 percent of all infants were born to women under twenty years old. "Childbearing at any age is a momentous event for a woman," the commission writes, "it is more so for a teenager, many of whom are unmarried. The strain, for both mother and child, is partially physical, but the burden is even greater from a social point of view."

Most of those actively involved in health care have always been surprised by the lack of interest with which the medical profession treats contraception. The report of the commission cites studies which show that private physicians, who provide the major share of health care in America, "do not perceive it to be their function to actively provide fertility control services. In part, this is because of the taboos that have historically surrounded fertility control. But it is also a result of the fact that our medical system primarily emphasizes curative medicine and acute, catastrophic care, rather than preventive medicine."

Until the 1950's family planning was hardly ever taught as a subject in medical school, and the only contact that one physician, who went on to devote a large part of his career to contraception, recalls having with birth control was an afternoon he spent at the Margaret Sanger Clinic in Manhattan. Today most medical schools are teaching family planning, but there are not enough physicians, nurses, and other specialized personnel to adequately staff family-planning services as well as to provide the closely related prenatal and postnatal care.

The commission mentions in this connection the fact that few health insurance plans pay for contraceptive services, and it recommends that "public and private health financing mechanisms should be paying the full cost of all services related to fertility, including contraceptive, prenatal, delivery, and postpartum services; pediatric care for the first year of life; voluntary sterilization; safe termination of unwanted pregnancy; and medical treatment of infertility."

Taking a look at the major social changes that are occurring today, the commission examines the effect that increased employment of women might have on the birth rate. Some experts believe that fertility will decrease as more women enter the job market. Others feel that the sex bias, low status, and poor pay that characterize many jobs held by women today will have to be remedied before employment will successfully compete with childbearing.

Higher education for women nevertheless is an important factor in depressing the fertility pattern of American women. Statistically, family size usually varies inversely with the education of the mother. The higher the education, the fewer the number of children. This is especially true of black and other minority women.

The commission is, however, careful in cautioning its audience against overzealousness.

Although we believed that increasing the freedom of women to seek alternative roles, may reduce fertility, this change is not sought on demographic grounds alone.

Here, as in the control of reproduction, our goal is to increase freedom of choice. Just as we oppose coercion in the control of fertility, we oppose any effort—explicitly or implicitly—to penalize childbearing and parenthood. We reject the notion that either motherhood or childlessness is or should be made to seem unfashionable. Instead, we seek a greater range of choice. Women should be able to choose motherhood, work, or other interests. Both men and women should be free to develop as individuals rather than being molded to fit some sexual stereotype.

The commission spent considerable time evaluating whether the birth rate of the United States could effectively be manipulated by a system of financial rewards or penalties. The present tax structure favors childbearing by the middle and upper-middle classes.

In this connection it might be interesting to note that contrary to popular belief, existing subsidies do not profit the prolific poor. Few federally funded housing projects, for instance, have apartments spacious enough to accommodate large families. There also is no increase in the number of children born to families who live in states with "good" welfare programs as compared to those who live in states with inadequate subsidies.

The commission examines various economic measures that might lower the birth rate. Programs such as not paying the educational costs for the third or higher birth-order child or levying a fee for childbearing are rejected outright because they either penalized the child or because they were deemed ineffectual. (The city-state of Singapore, which has one of the highest living standards of Southeast Asia coupled with a high birth rate, had just adopted such "punitive" measures.)

The U.S. commission also rejects direct financial rewards, such as paying $300 for not bearing a child or a larger sum for undergoing sterilization. "Bonus payments would serve to discourage childbearing only among the relatively few who are poorest," the commission states. "Therefore, it would not affect overall growth substantially, and would weigh unevenly upon decisions about childbearing in a manner we find unacceptable."

The conclusions reached by the Presidential commission make it clear that the population problem in the United States is crucial. As John D. Rockefeller III stated in his letter of transmission, the problem must be met in the traditional American way of "increasing public knowledge of the causes and consequences of population change, facilitating and guiding the processes of population movements, maximizing information about human reproduction and its consequences for the family, and enabling individuals to avoid unwanted fertility."

"No man is an island, intire of it selfe; every man is a peece of the Continent, a part of the maine; if Clod be washed away by the Sea, Europe is the lesse. . . ." John Donne wrote these lines almost four centuries ago, long before jet planes and instant communication welded the world into a small community.

Population problems in the impoverished, underdeveloped regions of the world are very different from those faced in the affluent United States, yet we may be able to learn a valuable lesson from countries that use different methods of health care. Of these, the People's Republic of China might very well be the most interesting, because China is one of the few nations that instead of emphasizing that having a small family might be a desirable personal goal, has stressed that the nation as a whole will suffer if people continue to have more than two children.

Until recently, China, which houses a fifth of the entire population of the earth, had a high birth rate. (Chinese demographic data is very unreliable. There is no official census, and population figures, except for cities, are a matter of estimates. Nevertheless, it is believed that the population of China increased from 530 million in 1948 to 800 million in 1970.)

In 1957 Chairman Mao expressed his wish to halt the population growth in China, but it is only since 1964 that the campaign has been in full swing. The Chinese goal is to reduce its annual population growth from more than 2 percent per year to 1 percent by 1985.

Dr. Victor Sidel, chief of the Department of Social Medicine at Montefiore Hospital in New York, and his author-wife, Ruth, recently visited China to examine at first hand how the Chinese are attempting to attain this goal.

The Chinese have always placed heavy emphasis on preventive medicine. As a matter of fact, one of the loveliest statements on the subject ever written was made almost five thousand years ago by Huang Ti, the Yellow Emperor of China:

Hence the sages did not treat those who were already ill; they instructed those who were not yet ill. . . . To administer medicines to diseases which have already developed and to suppress revolts which have already developed is comparable to the behavior of those persons who begin to dig a well after they have become thirsty, and of those who begin to cast weapons after they have already engaged in battle.

The present government of China has made family planning one of the most important aspects of preventive medicine. Preliminary data indicates that it is successful.

According to Dr. Sidel: "It works because the Chinese have couched the whole issue not in individual terms, but as an advantage to society as a whole. As with other medical problems, they mobilized the people in their own neighborhood to do the work."

In their efforts to limit fertility, the Chinese use the Pill, the IUD, condoms, tubal ligation, and vasectomies. The diaphragm has never been very popular. All contraceptive materials are manufactured in China. The country at present uses an oral contraceptive that must be taken during a period of twenty-two days, but a once-a-month pill is in an advanced experimental stage.

Abortions are freely available. As a matter of fact, the now widely used aspiration technique, developed by two Russian doctors in the 1920's, was kept alive by the "barefoot doctors" of China who used the portable equipment in rural areas. In addition to other social pressures and a clearly defined national goal, the Chinese at present also favor, and practice, late marriage. Extramarital sex is practically nonexistent.

As with other health measures, a large share of the fertility control program is carried out by nonphysician personnel. In the cities this includes Red Medical Workers, mostly housewives, who, according to Dr. Sidel, "teach by example." In rural areas information and the necessary materials are distributed by the "barefoot doctors" and midwives.

The current campaign has had excellent results in Shanghai, the only city for which there is solid demographic data. Matters might not work as well in rural areas where, as Chairman Mao told his old friend, the author and journalist Edgar Snow, "Women still believe that they must bear sons." Yet even if the final outcome of the Chinese effort is still in doubt, Dr. Sidel hopes that the Chinese example will convince others "that they must become involved in their own health care."

China's neighbor to the south, India, is another vast subcontinent with great population problems. According to Samuel Bunker, one of the Ford Foundation's experts on population problems who spends much of his time in India, "the numbers involved are so mind boggling that it is hard to conceive of them in real terms."

India supports 14 percent of the world's population on only 2.4 percent of the world's land. At present its population increases at the rate of one million persons every month. Such a growth rate offsets any improvement in the standard of living of the individual family, and as many persons have observed, conditions in the underdeveloped countries today are such that in spite of considerable technological advances, the poor are growing poorer.

The Indian government has made fertility control one of its prime objectives. Unlike China, the emphasis is on the benefit each individual family unit derives from being smaller.

Those who favor even limited controls feel that complete freedom of choice along these lines will not decrease birth rates. Others, impressed by the gently democratic ways of India, counter by stating that it is questionable that ideological considerations will affect the birth rate of the rural Chinese, whose educational level closely resembles that of rural India. At present there is no satisfactory answer to this question since demographic data for rural China is nonexistent.

The major problem in India, as elsewhere, is sociological. Nobody, as yet, has been able to convince the rural Indian couple that they are better off having only two children. According to Sam Bunker, "the rural Indian is so poor that the only thing he has is his family who provide him with respect, strength and security."

In spite of such odds the Indian government is spending a large amount of money on family planning. As a matter of fact, with 75,000 to 80,000 employees, the Family Planning Program is the second largest employer in India.

At present the program relies mainly on condoms, IUD's, and vasectomies. The Pill, so far, has not been approved for general use, partially because, as Mr. Bunker says, "India was badly burned with the IUD." Back in the 1960's when it was first developed, it was hailed as the solution to fertility problems in the underdeveloped countries. Experts were sent to India. Factories were built for the mass manufacture of Lippes' loops, and everybody hoped that India's population explosion was a thing of the past.

But the IUD, in India as elsewhere, was not as problem-free as expected. In a number of cases the device was associated with heavy bleeding, abdominal cramps, and unnoticed expulsion.

Consequently, India wants to proceed cautiously before it embarks on the mass distribution of another contraceptive device. The low dosage pill is being tested in pilot projects, and the government plans to use it on a wide scale in a couple of years.

The Indian effort, so far, has had little impact on the birth rate in rural communities, and some experts, like Roger Revelle of Harvard University, believe it will not level off until the infant death rate has dropped still further. Only then will the Indian couple believe that practically all their children will grow to adulthood. Dr. Revelle also hopes that increased material well-being will stimulate a desire for material possessions. This in turn may lead to a drop in the birth rate.

Even in India birth control has worked in small selected regions, such as the South Indian Tea Estates. This large industrial employer has paid 5 rupees a month—half the average daily wage—into savings accounts of female employees who have limited their family to two children. A third child "costs" the woman 50 rupees of her savings, a fourth 250. At age forty-five she receives the accumulated savings plus interest. So far, the program has been successful, and the birth rate in the Tea Estates has dropped.

Indian sterilization campaigns have also been effective. India has run several "vasectomy camps" staffed by twenty to fifty doctors and a large staff of supporting personnel. The camps were well publicized, and men who underwent the operation received some material goods and 110 rupees, which, as Sam Bunker says, "is probably more money than an average Indian ever has in his possession at any one time." One of the camps managed to perform sixty-five thousand vasectomies in one month, or two thousand in one day. Unfortunately, in India this is like the proverbial "drop in the bucket," especially since most patients already had fathered very large families.

Instead of rewards or ideological coercion, the South Asian city-state of Singapore, which, like Japan, has a high standard of living, has instituted punitive measures. In November 1972, the health minister announced that "for Singapore in the 1970's, the third child is a luxury and the fourth and fifth anti-social acts." The measure, which has just gone into effect, provides lower income taxes for families with only three children, lower priority for government housing for large families, and increasingly high maternity fees for higher birth-order children.

India, China, the United States, Singapore, and lessons learned from history make it clear that there is much more to family planning than good methods of birth control. Family size, on a worldwide scale, has become a public health issue. Those who are disturbed by the thought that any regulation, no matter how indirect, of the number of children each couple should bear is an interference with personal freedom must remember that freedom has always been subject to the overriding and changing needs of society: We submit to all kinds of laws today that former generations might have considered as an infringement of their liberty.

Not so long ago, for instance, it was assumed that whether a person had smallpox was his own affair; nor was his right questioned to run his carriage down the middle of the road or to dump his garbage wherever he pleased. Though a citizen even today may consider restrictions in these matters a bother, the realization that they contribute to his own freedom makes most comply without a murmur.

Even though the population explosion is the most urgent problem we are facing today, it would be wrong to leave the reader with the impression that fertility control by itself would resolve all of mankind's ills. Fewer people will simply give mankind a breathing spell. This view is shared by Dr. Herman P. Miller, chief of the Population Division of the U.S. Bureau of the Census, who stated in 1970:

What we need is a national commitment to use our growing affluence to attack our domestic problems. Nothing less will do. The choice is ours. If we choose to spend our money on wars, our ability to deal with domestic problems will be seriously impaired. If we choose to invest in space exploration, we may solve all of the mysteries of the universe and remain ignorant about man himself. If we choose to give ourselves tax cuts, we will spend the money on things we can buy—more material goods which will intensify many of our problems. If we choose to spend more of our money for public services, then we might buy pure air and water, cleaner and more efficient transportation systems, better schools, the elimination of hunger and the reduction of poverty.

Conclusion

Most people will use contraceptives during part of their lives. Even though medicine has not yet come up with a perfect solution, few people need to have unwanted pregnancies.

Not all contraceptives are good for everybody. Life styles, medical considerations, and personal preferences play an important part in the choice of a method. Needs may also change with time. A tubal ligation or vasectomy may be ideal for the husband and wife who have had all the children they want, but it is probably unsuitable for a pair of college students.

Each person must carefully choose the type of birth-control method he or she is comfortable with. Sometimes this means trying more than one technique.

Those who consider this a nuisance should remember how much time is spent on finding the right kind of diet, the perfect shampoo, the best headache remedy, or a suitable set of clothes.

The effectiveness and most obvious advantages and disadvantages of each type are given on page 141.

COMMON CONTRACEPTIVE METHODS

METHOD	EFFECTIVENESS	ADVANTAGES	DISADVANTAGES
COITUS INTERRUPTUS	Variable.		Nuisance, great psychological strain for male partner.
CONDOM	98% when used alone. Better when used in conjunction with spermicidal jelly or vaginal foam.	Only used when needed. Easy to use. No physiological effect. Freely available.	Nuisance.
DIAPHRAGM	90% effective. More so when used with adequate amount of spermicidal jelly.	Only used when needed. No physiological effect.	Requires care and preparation. Must be fitted by qualified medical personnel.
IUD	98%	One-time decision. No systemic physiological effect. No preparation.	Some women have heavy periods and cramps. Must be inserted by qualified medical personnel. Cannot be used by everybody.
ORAL CONTRACEPTIVES (THE PILL)	100% when taken as prescribed.	No preparation.	Increases frequency of thromboembolic disease. Long-term physiological effects unknown. Weight gain, morning sickness during early usage.
VAGINAL FOAM	Not very effective.	Only used when needed. Freely available.	Must be applied before sexual intercourse.

Bibliography

Corner, G. W., *Anatomist at Large*. New York: Basic Books, 1958.

—— *The Hormones in Human Reproduction*. London: Oxford Press, 1963.

Demarest, R. J. and Sciarra, J. J., *Conception, Birth and Contraception*. New York: McGraw-Hill, Inc., 1969.

Ehrlich, P. R., *The Population Bomb*. New York: Sierra Club/Ballantine Books, Inc., 1968.

Finch, B. L. and Green, Hugh, *Conception Through the Ages*. Springfield,

Illinois: Charles C Thomas, Publisher, 1963.

Fryer, Peter, *The Birth Controllers*. New York: Stein & Day, Publishers, 1966.

Green, Shirley, *The Curious History of Contraception*. London: Ebury Press, 1971.

Guttmacher, A. F., *Pregnancy, Birth and Family Planning*. New York: The Viking Press, Inc., 1973.

Hardin, Garrett, *Population, Evolution, Birth Control*. San Francisco: W. H. Freeman and Company.

Havemann, Ernest, *Birth Control*. New York: Time-Life Books, 1967.

Himes, N. E., *Medical History of Contraception*. New York, Gamut Press, 1963.

Maisel, A. Q., *The Hormone Quest*. New York: Random House, Inc., 1965.

Malthus, Thomas, *On Population*. New York: The Modern Library, Inc., 1960.

Rock, John, *The Time Has Come*. New York: Alfred A. Knopf, Inc., 1963.

Sanger, Margaret, *An Autobiography*. New York: W. W. Norton & Company, Inc., 1938.

Westoff, L. A. and Westoff, C. F., *From Now to Zero*. Boston: Little, Brown and Company, 1968.

Population & the American Future, The Report of the Commission on Population Growth. New York: Signet, 1972.

Index

Abortion, methods and practice,
112–14
aspiration (vacuum) technique,
114–15
case history, 19–21
D and C, 114
drug-induced, 115–16
legal aspects, 117
self-induced, 114
socioeconomic aspects, 80–81,
111–17
Allen, Edgar, 55
Allen, Willard M., 56
Alpha-chlorohydrin, 106
*American Journal of Obstetrics
and Gynecology*, 88
Aquapendente, Fabricius ab, 37
Aschheim, Selmar, 54, 87
Aschheim-Zondek test, 54, 57
Aspiration technique (abortion),
114–15
Association for Voluntary
Sterilization, 109

"Band-Aid" surgery (tubal liga-
tion), 109
Banting, Frederick, 58
Bayliss, William Maddock, 52, 59
Beasley, Joseph Diehl, 4, 5, 10, 11,
34
Bedford, Michael, 106, 107
"Belly button" surgery (tubal liga-
tion), 109
Bernard, Claude, 51–52
Berthold, Arnold Adolph, 50–51, 52
Best, Charles, 58
Biological cycles, 48–49. *See also*
Reproduction
Birth control. *See* Contraception
Birth Control Review, 32

Birth rate (*see also* Population
Growth)
abortion and, 116
culture and, 9
government and, 126–39
IUD effect on, 95
socioeconomic aspects of, 5–6,
82
Blackmun, Harry A., 111–12
Bloch, Anita, 17
Boccaccio, 4
Bouton, Jim, 108
Brave New World (Huxley), 73
"Breakthrough" bleeding, 75
Breast-feeding, conception and, 9
Bryman, Ethel, 28, 31
Bucalo, Louis, 109
Brinker, Samuel, 135, 136, 137
Bureau of Census, U. S., 138
Butenandt, Adolph, 57

Cancer, IUD use and, 94
Capacitation, 107
Casanova, 98
Castration, 49
pituitary glands and, 53
Call, The (Socialist newspaper),
12, 17
Chang, Min-Chueh, 70–71, 75, 76
Chile, abortions and birth rates in,
113–14
Clinics, birth-control, 5–6
first, 28–30
Clyman, Martin, 109
Coitus interruptus, 96
Commission on Population
Growth and the American Fu-
ture, 128–33
Comstock, Anthony, 18, 22
Comstock Law, 18, 23

Condoms, development and use, 97–102
Contraception, methods, and practice (*see also specific methods*; Birth rate; Population growth; Reproduction)
  ancient, 6–9, 96–98
  categories, 6
  common (chart), 140
  ignorance and, 4–5
  in males, 96–110
  Margaret Sanger and, 13–34
  legal and religious aspects, 11–12, 96–97
  modern, 11
  socioeconomic aspects, 125
  technological developments, 11, 118–25
  traditional, 11
  turn-of-the-century devices, 25
Corner, George Washington, 56
Corpus luteum, 56, 57
  contraceptive research and, 120
Cortisone, 62
Crane, Frederick E., 32
Creams, contraceptive, 121
Culture, birth rate and, 9
Cu-7 IUD, 122

Darrow, Clarence, 26
Decameron (Boccaccio), 4
De Graaf, Regnier, 40–42, 44, 45, 51, 56
Diaphragms, 67, 120, 121
  development of, 26
Dickinson, Robert L., 88
Dilation and curettage (D and C), 83, 114
Diosgenin, 61, 64
Doisy, Edward, 55
Dollinger, J., 42
Donne, John, 133
Douches, 23
Drugs (*see also* Oral Contraceptives; Pill, The)

Drugs:
  contraceptive, 6
  inducing abortions and, 115–16

Ehrlich, Paul, 108
Eisenhower, Dwight D., 3
Eliezer, Rabbi, 97
Ellis, Havelock, 23
Embryology, mammalian, 35–47
Endometrium, 57
Enovid, 78
Epididymis, 102, 104
Ericsson, R. J., 106
Estrogen, 55, 67, 68, 69
Estrogens, 55, 107
Esterone, 55
Estradiol, 55

Fallopius, Gabriel, 36, 37, 97
Family Limitation (pamphlet), 23
Fertility, 82, 107
  contraceptive methods and, 9
  (*See also* Rhythm)
Fertilization, 44, 57
France, 22, 23
Freschi, Judge, 30
FSH (follicle-stimulating hormone), 53, 57, 58, 67, 68, 69, 104, 124, 125

Gandhi, Indira, 128
Garcia, Celso Ramon de, 77
Gegenbaur, Karl, 46
Generatione Animalium, De (Harvey), 37, 39
Girardin, Marc, 51
Goldstein, Jonah J., 30, 32
Gonadotropic hormones, 53
Government, contraception and birth-control information, 5, 29–34
  population growth and, 126–39
  regulation, 11–12
Graefenberg, Ernst, 83, 86–87, 89, 122
"Graffian follicles," 42
Guttmacher, Alan F., 19, 80–83, 89, 90, 93, 114

Halban, Josef, 54
Hall, Herbert H., 88, 89
Halton, Mary, 88
Harvey, William, 37–39, 41, 44, 49
Hertig, Arthur T., 73
Higgins, Michael Hennessey, 13–14
Hormones, physiology and function, 52–55, 58, 59 (see also specific names)
  in menstrual cycle, 58, 68–69
  in spermatogenesis, 104, 107
  synthetic, 60–64, 76–77
Huang Ti, 134
Human Fertility (periodical), 88
Humani Corporis Fabrica, De (Versalius), 36
Huxley, Aldous, 73
Hypothalmus, contraception research and, 124–25

ICSH (interstitial cell-stimulating hormone), 53
India, population growth problems in, 135–37
Infertility, 73–77
International Congress on Intrauterine Contraception, 89, 92
In vitro fertilization, 73
Ishihama, Atsumi, 89
IUD (intrauterine device)
  development and use, 83–95
  modern, 91
  pessaries, 85
  research, 122
  size, 84
  technological advances, 120
  types, 94

Jackson, Margaret, 89
Jacobs, Aletta, 26
Jellies, contraceptive, 121
Johnson, Lyndon B., 128

Kaplan, Harvey, 124
Knauer, Emil, 54

Leeuwenhoek, Anton van, 39–40, 41, 101
Lehfeldt, Hans, 87
Lehmann, Frederick, 62
Levene, P. A., 60
LH (lutenizing hormone), 53, 57, 58, 69, 104, 124, 125
Lippes, Jack, 92
Lippes loop, 92
Loeb, Leo, 56

"Male pill," 105–106
Malpighi, Marcello, 41
Malthus, Thomas Robert, 3, 23–24, 128
Mao Tse-tung, 128, 134, 135
Margulies, Lazar C., 90, 92
Marker, Russell, 59–64
Mechanical devices, contraceptive, 6 (see also IUD)
  as abortion alternative, 116
  effectiveness, 9
  120
  research and development, turn-of-the-century, 25
Medical profession, attitude toward contraception, 6
Medroxyprogesterone acetate, 120
Menkin, Miriam F., 73
Mensinga, Wilhelm, 26
Mensinga diaphragm, 26
Menstrual extraction, 124
Menstruation, anatomy and physiology, 57 (see also Reproduction)
  cycle, 68–69
  mini-pill and, 119
  ovulation and, 9
  hormones and, 58
Merck and Co., 62
Miller, Herman P., 138
Mindell, Fania, 28
"Mini-pill," 119
Miscarriage, spontaneous, 114
"Morning after" pill, 107
Motu Cordes, De (Harvey), 37
Mussalam, Basim, 127, 128

National Socialists, 87
National Woman's Health Coalition, 124
Neo-Malthusian League, 23
Netherlands (Holland), 26
Nidation, 57
Nixon, Richard M., 128
Nony-g (nonylphenoxypolyethoxyethanol), 121
Norethynodrel, 78
Notestern, Frank W., 89, 94

Office of Population Research, U. S., 125
Oppenheimer, W., 88–89
Oral contraceptives, development and use, 6, 9, 67 (see also Pill, The)
  population growth and, 82
  research in, 118–20
Oster, Gerald, 123
Ota, Dr., 89
Ovulation, anatomy and physiology, 55, 68, 69 (see also Menstruation; Reproduction)
  research in predicting, 122–23

Parke-Davis, 60, 61
Pelvic infections, IUD use and, 94
People's Republic of China, population growth problems and solutions, 133–36
Pessaries, 23, 83, 85
"Phasers" (vasectomy), 109
Pill, The (see also Oral contraceptives)
  development, 67, 69–79
  effectiveness, 116
  new research, 119–20
  testing, 77–79
Pincus, Gregory, 65–67, 69, 71, 74, 75, 76, 118
Pituitary gland, physiology and function, 52–53, 58, 67
Planned Parenthood Association, 96
Population Council, 89

Population growth, socioeconomic aspects (see also Birth rate)
  as a global problem, 1–3, 82, 138–39
  history of, 126–28
  in India, 136–37
  in People's Republic of China, 133–36
  in Singapore, 137
  in United States, 128–33
Postcoital pills, 107
Pregnancy, teen-age, 116
  wanted vs. unwanted, 116–17
Prenant, Louis Auguste, 56
Progesterone, physiology and function, 56, 57, 61, 62, 69, 71, 75
Progestin, 107
Progestins, 76–77
Prostaglandins, abortions and, 114
Puerto Rico, testing The Pill in, 77–79
Pust, Karl, 83
Pust pessaries, 83, 85

Religion, abortion and, 117
Rembrandt, 41
Reproduction, anatomy and physiology, 48–64 (see also Contraception)
  breast-feeding and, 9
  contraceptive research and, 123–24
  effectiveness of contraceptive measures and, 9, 11
  female cycle, 55, 57
  history of knowledge about, 35–47
  ignorance about, 4
  male, 57–58
  rhythm method and, 9, 11
  spermatogenesis, 102–105
Revelle, Roger, 136
Rhythm method, contraception and, 6, 9, 75, 123
  menstrual cycle and, 11

Rock, John, 11, 71–75, 90
Rockefeller, John D. III, 89, 128,
  133
Roman Catholic Church
  abortion attitude, 117
  contraception attitude, 9, 34, 74,
  75
Rosenkranz, George, 62
Royal Society of London, 39, 40
Rutgers, Johannes, 26

"Safe period," 9, 11
Salves, contraceptive, 122
Sanger, Bill, 16
Sanger, Margaret, 12, 13–34, 66–
  67, 87, 96, 114, 118
Sapogenins, 61
Scheer, Irving, 121, 122
Schleiden, M. J., 46
Schwann, Theodor, 46
Searle and Co., 76
Secretin, 52
Segal, Sheldon J., 89, 119, 120
Seminal fluid, 104
Seminiferous tubule, 102, 104
Sidel, Victor, 134, 135
Silastic capsule, contraceptive re-
  search and, 119
Singapore, population growth
  problems and solutions, 137
Snow, Edgar, 135
Society for the Suppression of
  Vice, 18
Somlo, Emeric, 62
Spermatazoa, 46–47
  cells, 101, 103
  discovery of, 40
Spermatogenesis, anatomy and
  physiology, 102–105
  halting, 105–108
Sperm banks, 108
Spermicidal chemicals, 121–22
"Spit test" (ovulation), 123
Sponges, contraceptive, 23
Starling, Ernest Henry, 52, 59
Stem pessaries, 83, 85
Sterility, testosterone and, 105

Sterilization
  tubal ligation, 109–10
  vasectomy, 108–109
Steroids, hormones and, 60–64
Stone, Abraham, 67, 78
Suppositories, contraceptive, 23
Supreme Court, 117
  abortion decision, 111–12
Syntex Sociédad Anonima, 62

Talmud, 9
Tatum, Howard J., 122
Testosterone, physiology and
  function, 56, 57, 61, 104–105,
  125
Testes, physiology and function,
  49–51, 52, 104
Therapeutic abortions, 116–17
Tietze, Christopher, 88, 89, 93, 94,
  115
Tubal ligation, 109

"Unisex" pill, 125
United States, population growth
  problems, 128–33
University of Leyden, 41
Uterine infections, 86

Vaccines, spermatogenesis and,
  108
Vacuum abortion, 115
Vas deferens, 102, 104
Vasectomy, methods and practice,
  108–109
  in India, 137
Venereal disease, condom use
  and, 97–101
Vesalius, Andreas, 36, 37
von Baer, Karl Ernst, 42–46, 65
von Kölliker, Albert, 46

Woman Rebel, The (Sanger pamphlet), 23

Zinsser, Hans, 109
Zipper, Jaime, 122
Zondek, Bernhard, 54, 87